D1153031

MSU
LIBRARIES

RETURNING MATERIALS:
Place in book drop to
remove this checkout from
your record.   FINES will
be charged
retur

YOUR CAREER IN
OFFICE
OCCUPATIONS

SEP 1978

arco's
CAREER GUIDANCE SERIES

YOUR CAREER IN
OFFICE
OCCUPATIONS

Gilbert Klevins

ARCO PUBLISHING COMPANY, INC.
219 Park Avenue South, New York, N.Y. 10003

Produced by Cal Industries, Inc.
76 Madison Avenue, New York, N.Y. 10016

Published by Arco Publishing Company, Inc.
219 Park Avenue South, New York, N.Y. 10003

Copyright © 1978 by Cal Industries, Inc.

All rights reserved. No part of this book may be
reproduced, by any means, without permission in
writing from the publisher, except by a reviewer
who wishes to quote brief excerpts in connection
with a review in a magazine or newspaper.

Library of Congress Cataloging in Publication Data

Klevins, Gil.
   Your career in office occupations.

   (Arco's career guidance series)
   Bibliography: p. 117
   1. Clerical occupations. I. Title.

HF5501.K57   651'.374'023   77-17377
ISBN 0-668-04449-7 (Library Edition)
ISBN 0-668-04434-9 (Paper Edition)

Printed in the United States of America

3576850

Have you ever considered how much our daily lives depend on office workers? Whether we receive a letter, go shopping, cash a paycheck, or travel, we need the services of efficient and reliable workers.

If you add up all the people involved in the services you and I need every day, it becomes no surprise to learn that one job in every six is an office job. And without office employees, corporations, stores, hotels, and even the government could not function.

Some office employees enjoy working with customers in person or over the phone; other office employees enjoy more solitary work. Whichever your preference, you can find a challenging career in office work.

Many organizations sponsor training programs. These training programs can help employees to further develop their office skills, or to understand and work with computers, or to become supervisors and managers. In short, such training helps you *and* your employer.

ARCO publishing has produced this book to help you decide on the type of office work you would like to do. This book tells you what is done on the job, what personal abilities and skills are required, what opportunities exist, how to get a job, and what salary, benefits and working conditions to expect.

William J. Ninehan
Assistant Treasurer and Manager of Instruction
Bankers Trust Company
New York, New York 10006

CONTENTS

INTRODUCTION

Over 15 million people, more than 17 percent of the total workforce, are currently engaged in office work of one kind or another. That is a considerable slice of the working population, a slice that is expected to grow faster than the average for all occupations throughout the next ten years.

Not only these numbers, but also the diversity and possibility for advancement offer opportunities for the job-seeker. Almost without exception (regardless of one's interests and aptitudes), a suitable position exists in the field of office occupations.

These jobs are available, but there are, of course, some requirements. Virtually all employers require high school diplomas and, in some cases, further education and training. Before applying for a job, technical secretaries, for example, must have a basic knowledge of the particular field they wish to enter. Additional training will be received on the job, but a strong foundation of knowledge must already exist. This advanced training can be obtained at a specialized business or technical school or at a college or university.

If a particular office occupation appeals to you, and you believe you have the aptitude for it, a course of study in high school can usually be found or devised to aid you in achieving your goal. The career or guidance counselor should be able to suggest specific classes which will best meet your needs.

Although all office workers receive some on-the-job training (either in the particular area in which they are involved, in general office procedure, or in office procedure "the way we do it around here"), there are certain abilities and skills which all (with the noted exceptions) seekers of office jobs would do well to have. These are:

- A frame of mind in which the job is taken seriously.

- The desire to do the job to the best of one's ability.

- A neat appearance.

- An attentiveness to detail.

- A preference for indoor work.

- The ability to remain seated during most of the work day. (The exceptions to this are stock clerks and shipping and receiving clerks.)

- The ability to type. (This is not actually *necessary* for positions other than secretary, stenographer, and typist, but it is definitely an asset.)

- A basic knowledge of filing and general office practices.

- The ability to do simple math.

- The ability to communicate effectively in both verbal and written English. (This includes a proficiency in grammar, spelling, and vocabulary.)

Although the impact of automation on office occupations is greater in some areas than in others, training and/or experience with automated equipment can be important to advancement. As more and more tasks become automated, more and more supervisors are likely to be chosen from the ranks of those who are familiar with new methods and machines. Even if the particular position is not directly involved with this equipment, employers will want managers and supervisors who, in their indirect dealings with the machines, will be able to function comfortably and proficiently.

Just as there are numerous office occupations from which to choose, so are there a variety of organizations. This means not only choosing the field in which one would like to work (insurance, publishing, etc.), but also the size of the organization and its location.

Workers in large offices usually do not have to have as broad a knowledge of office procedures or as wide a range of skills as the worker in a small organization. A beginning bookkeeper in a large accounting or bookkeeping department, for example, is generally assigned one specific task. On the other hand, the bookkeeper in a small organization, especially if he or she is the only bookkeeper employed, must have the kind of wide and thorough knowledge which will allow him or her to take care of all of the company's books.

Personality is also a factor in choosing the size of the organization. Someone who prefers having a lot of people around will naturally feel more comfortable in a large office, and someone who likes working alone will prefer a smaller organization.

Objectively, the basic advantages of a large organization over a small one are the fact that the salary is generally higher, the benefits more extensive, and, perhaps most important of all, there is the possibility of advancement within the company.

Most people are not able to move to another area in order to work in preferable surroundings. In most cases people go where the work is, nearest to wherever they happen to be living. However, there is a certain amount of choice possible even in these circumstances, and it is wise to give some thought to the matter before embarking on a job hunt.

One of the largest employers of entry-level office personnel is the government: federal, state, and local. The advantages of working for government are a higher starting salary than one can expect in the private sector, job security, and (on the federal level) the possibility of an overseas assignment. The disadvantages are a top salary beyond which one can usually not go, slow advancement, and the fact that overseas assignments are few and most often given to "senior" employees.

Unless one is employed as a stock clerk or shipping and receiving clerk (in which case one may not work in particularly pleasant surroundings), working conditions for most office occupations are fairly comfortable.

Benefits, although they do vary somewhat from one company to another, have been standardized to a degree in the areas of vacations and sick days. (Check the particular chapter for specifics.)

Salary varies enormously depending upon position, training and experience, and the amount of responsibility which the job entails.

1 The BANK TELLER

Bank tellers cash checks, process checking and savings account transactions, sell money orders, accept credit card and loan payments, sell food stamps, and accept payments for utility bills.

All banks have at least two things in common: money and tellers, and without tellers, the banks would have no money. Oh, you might say, but other bank employees could accept deposits, cash checks, and perform the functions done by tellers. That is true, but then they would, in effect, be tellers. The point is that tellers are indispensable to the operation of any bank.

The size of the bank, or branch, and the amount of business transacted determine the number of tellers. In a small branch, one "all-round" teller, or **unit teller**, is responsible for handling all transactions. Larger or busier branches may have a number of all-round tellers or they may have different kinds of tellers to handle different transactions.

Currently, there are approximately 300,000 tellers working in commercial and savings banks in the United States. Many of these work on a part-time or per diem (by the day) basis. Part-time tellers work a few hours each day, usually during the lunch hour when traffic in the bank is heaviest. Per diem tellers work a minimum of two full days each week. Although most part-time and per diem tellers work in the same bank every day, some are hired as "floaters." Floaters move from bank to bank in a particular area, generally filling-in for tellers who are ill or on vacation. Because banks have found that the system of hiring part-time and per diem tellers works so well, the trend in banking is toward hiring more such tellers. It might seem that this will diminish the number of full-time positions available; however, as the total number of tellers is expected to increase, the current balance should be maintained. Also to be considered is the fact that the content of the training program is the same for full-time, part-time, and per diem tellers. Thus, even if a full-time position is not immediately available, there is the possibility of obtaining such a post after having worked for a while in a part-time or per diem capacity.

WHAT DOES A BANK TELLER DO?

Although there are different types of tellers, unit tellers are the most common. Unit tellers are trained to handle most of the transactions which take place at a bank "window."

Many of these transactions use checks. A check is an order instructing the bank to pay a specified amount to the person or company to whom the check is issued. The most common types of checks are personal and business checks, certified checks, which are stamped by the bank, certifying that the funds are available in the account on which the check is drawn, and cashier's checks (also called *bank checks* because the check is bought from the bank, thus, when the check is cashed, the money is drawn directly from the bank's funds). Money orders are similar to cashier's checks, as they are purchased from the bank.

Unit tellers are trained to cash checks, accept deposits (in cash or check) after making sure that the checks have been endorsed and that the amount entered on the deposit slip is accurate, process savings deposits and withdrawals, and sell money orders. In order to be able to handle these transactions, a teller must learn to check balances (the amount currently on deposit with the bank in that account) to make sure that there is enough money available in the account to pay the check, confirm signatures to make sure that the check has been written by the person (or persons) authorized to use the account, and examine cash deposits to be certain that the bills are not counterfeit.

More experienced tellers, such as **note tellers,** may accept credit card and utility bill payments, sell food stamps, issue cash advances on credit cards, sell traveler's checks, and deal with some foreign checks and currency.

Most tellers use adding machines to help with the math involved in transactions. Tellers who process savings may use a "window" posting machine, which prints a receipt for the deposit, enters the amount in the customer's passbook, and enters the transaction in the bank's ledger. Many banks are adopting the use of data processing equipment. Terminals installed at each window automatically perform many duties (such as checking balances) which tellers must do manually.

At the end of the day, each teller must make accounts balance.

SKILL/PERSONALITY CHECKLIST

The following questions are designed to help you evaluate whether or not your abilities and personality indicate an aptitude for a position as a bank teller. This is not, however, the last word; you should merely regard the result as an indication of your *present* status in relation to this position. This is not a test which you will either pass or fail. Answer the questions honestly, as your answers will help you determine the most suitable course for your future.

Respond to the questions in the following manner: **1** = little or no skill; **2** = moderate skill; **3** = superior skill. The questions relating to personality cannot, of course, be answered on the basis of skill; respond to them numerically, as the others, on the basis of degree (**1** = little or none; **2** = moderate; **3** = superior).

A total of between **12** and **19** indicates little or no aptitude for work as a bank teller; **20-28**, moderate aptitude; **29-36**, superior aptitude.

☐ Are you reliable?

☐ Are you willing to take the job seriously?

☐ How well do you organize?

☐ How proficient are you in addition and subtraction?

☐ Can you alphabetize?

☐ Are you familiar with any filing system?

☐ Can you operate an adding machine?

☐ Do you have any knowledge of bookkeeping or accounting?

☐ Are you familiar with any data processing systems?

☐ Do you prefer indoor to outdoor work?

☐ Are you usually courteous?

☐ Are you able to react calmly to people who are upset or impatient?

SKILLS AND PERSONALITY

Reliability is the cornerstone of a position as a bank teller. This means appearing for work on time, neatly groomed and dressed. But it is not only that. Nor does it just apply to one's honesty. It also applies to proficiency and professionalism. Reliability means exactly what it says, the ability to be relied upon. A bank teller must realize that he or she has a responsibility both to the bank and to the bank's customers. This is a part of taking the job seriously. Banks want employees who recognize the position of trust for which they have been engaged.

Dealing with money and checks requires **organization.** Transactions must be handled in an orderly fashion, accounts must be checked carefully, signatures verified carefully; and all in the correct sequence. If the position of bank teller appeals to you, but you think you do things in a rather casual way, now is the time to begin cultivating orderly habits.

Much of a teller's workday is devoted to the **addition and subtraction** of figures. You should be able to do so fairly rapidly and quite accurately. Of course, you will have an adding machine to help in your computations, but doing the simple problems by hand is often faster.

You must be able to **alphabetize.** Every time you are asked to cash a check, you will have to compare the signature on the check with the signature card in the bank's files. In order to do this, you will have to be familiar with alphabetization. Although you will probably not be called upon to alphabetize a stack of cards, you will have to be able to find the proper card quickly and return it to its correct place in the files.

The orderly **filing** of papers is as important in a bank as it is in any other business. You may not know the filing system used by the bank, but familiarity with any filing system will make it that much easier for you to learn whatever system is used by the bank.

During the training course (if the bank offers one) or during on-the-job training, you will learn how to **use an adding machine.** However, if you already have this skill when applying for a job, that ability will be considered a point in your favor. If two individuals apply for a position at a bank and both have the same qualifications, except that one can operate an adding machine and the other cannot, the one who has the skill will probably get the job.

Knowing how to use an adding machine is a valuable skill when applying for a position as a bank teller.

Like filing and using an adding machine, a knowledge of **bookkeeping** or accounting is not absolutely necessary when applying for a job as a bank teller. However, like those two, it is something which the personnel manager will consider an asset. Knowledge in this area will also help you to obtain promotions once you have been hired. You will, of course, be able to learn while you are working, but having this knowledge before you apply will put you that much further ahead.

More and more banks are relying on data processing systems for storing information and handling such routine functions as checking balances. In most cases, a terminal (a keyboard which is used for asking the computer for information) is installed at each teller's window. These terminals are connected to a central unit (sometimes located at the bank's main office) in which the information is stored and from which the information requested is transmitted to the teller. Once again, the operation of these machines will be taught during training, but if you have the opportunity to learn a bit about data processing systems and their operation, the knowledge will be considered a point in your favor when applying for a teller's position.

Electronic data processing is essential to operations.

Banks are service businesses. They are involved in selling a function rather than a product which can be touched. Since, to a great extent, all banks sell the same services, one of the few things which make one bank more appealing to potential customers than another is the **courtesy** of its employees. This has become of major importance to banks which, today, are energetically competing for a greater share of the available business. Consequently, one of the qualities banks look for when hiring tellers is courtesy. Lack of courtesy might cause a customer to move his account to another bank and might also cause the discourteous teller to lose his job. This is something to remember when applying for a job, during formal or on-the-job training and when you have actually begun working.

The ability to react calmly to people who are upset or impatient is actually a part of courtesy. But because this situation occurs so frequently in banks (particularly during busy hours), it deserves special mention. When banks become crowded and the waiting lines are long, customers tend to become impatient and sometimes angry, especially if they happen to be on their lunch hour. Although they should understand that things are moving as quickly as possible and wait patiently, they often do not. Not only does it not help to return anger when a customer is unpleasant (in fact, it may provoke the customer even more), it also produces a bad impression should one of your superiors overhear you. You should, instead, try to be pleasant and explain that this is a busy time of day. You might, in addition say that you are sorry they had to wait so long. Not everyone will appreciate your apology, but most people will react favorably.

WHAT ARE THE OPPORTUNITIES?

The number of tellers needed in the banking industry is expected to increase faster than the average of all occupations during the next five to ten years. Many of these, as previously mentioned, will be part-time and per diem employees. However, there will still be a considerable number of full-time teller positions available.

Formal training programs for full-time tellers usually last about two weeks. Programs for part-time and per diem tellers are generally shorter (about nine days), although instructors try to cover the same material. (There is currently a movement to extend part-time and per diem training, since those workers are expected to perform the same tasks even though they work a shorter period.) On-the-job training is, of course, longer since there is less time available each day for instruction.

Although there are private training schools for tellers (as well as some federally funded programs which, basically, do little more than prepare a person to apply for a teller's job), anyone who is hired as a teller is required to go through the training program regardless of prior instruction. Thus, attending a private school is not really worthwhile.

After completing the training program, tellers are considered trainees for three months to one year (the length of time depends upon the progress of the individual). The experienced teller is then able to advance him/herself through additional on-the-job training or advanced courses, if they are offered by the bank. Among the positions which may be obtained in this way are **note teller, international clerk,** and **teller supervisor.** Although the teller supervisor also works at a window, he/she has additional responsibilities: the person to whom all the other tellers report and liaison between the tellers and management. All tellers advance in "grade" (with an accompanying increase in salary), but this is based on the length of time one has been employed.

Some banks offer **platform assistant programs** in which one can gain the knowledge necessary for this position. Management development programs are also offered by some banks, and through these one may "come up from the ranks" to a management position. However, there are some banks which require their management personnel to have college degrees.

Almost every bank has an education program. If a bank employee wishes to go to school, if the classes taken are work-related, and if a grade of "C" or better is obtained, the bank will pay the cost of the classes. An employee may also take advantage of this program even if the classes are not work-related, provided he or she is working toward a college degree. In this way a teller may, without cost, earn the degree which some banks require for promotion to a management position. If the employee does not have the money needed (since the bank will not pay the cost of the class until a grade has been received), the employee may take out a loan at an extremely low rate of interest and pay it back when the bank is satisfied that an acceptable grade has been obtained.

GETTING A JOB AS A BANK TELLER

Although it may seem like a superficial aspect, an important thing to remember when applying for a position as a bank teller (or for any position in business) is to "look the part." Before you are judged on any other basis, you will be judged on the basis of your appearance. A male teller is expected to wear a coat and tie. A female teller is expected to be neatly and fairly conservatively dressed (no hats or kerchiefs may be worn on the job). Jeans, even if they are very expensive jeans, are not permitted to be worn by either men or women. These dress codes may not appeal to you, but they are the standards observed in most banks, and if you want to work as a teller, you must conform to them. This applies not only after you have been hired, but also when you apply for the position and during the training period, even if the training is conducted in a classroom

Punctuality is something else which must be remembered during application, training, and employment. If you have a two-o'clock appointment with the personnel manager, be there at two o'clock. If, while in training, you are given an hour for lunch, return to class in an hour. (Remember, you have already been hired and are being paid full wages, and you can be fired.) Naturally, punctuality is important once you actually begin working in the bank; you are an integral part of the bank's operation. If you are not there, everything slows down.

Every bank employee is bonded. Being bonded means that a bonding company guarantees the honesty of the bonded individual and agrees to pay a certain amount should the bank suffer any financial loss because of that person's dishonesty.

This is not something which should worry you, but since the interviewer will probably ask if you have ever been bonded, or if you have ever been denied bond, it is something of which you should be aware.

SALARY, BENEFITS, AND WORKING CONDITIONS

The average salary for full-time, beginning bank tellers is $130 per week. The average for per diem workers is $26 per day. And the average for part-time tellers is $3.70 per hour. Each teller is reviewed after having been employed for between six months and one year, and a raise is usually given at that time based upon the quality of the teller's performance. Further reviews occur approximately once each year, and the raises given at those times are also based upon performance.

Most banks give a maximum of eleven paid holidays per year. However, if only nine holidays fall on working days, nine holidays are all that are allowed. There is usually no specific number of "sick days" allowed. If you are ill or cannot come to work for some other justifiable reason, it is, of course, permitted so long as you notify the bank. "Excessive" or "regular" absences from work, however, are not permitted. Two additional days per year are generally allowed for the employee's personal business (doctor, dentist, etc.) or the observance of a religious holiday.

Like most other businesses, banks give their employees two weeks paid vacation after one year on the job, three weeks after five years, and four weeks after ten years.

Additional benefits include free checking accounts (if you work for a commercial bank rather than one which deals only in savings), free traveler's checks, easily obtainable loans, and medical insurance. Most banks also offer pension plans to which the employee may contribute (in addition to the amount contributed by the bank). There is usually a choice of pension plans, each of which should be considered in relation to one's individual plans. By far the greatest benefit, however, is the educational program; it is an excellent opportunity to increase an understanding of the banking field as well as one's general store of knowledge.

2 The BOOKKEEPER

Bookkeepers maintain up-to-date records of money owed the company, bills to be paid, assets, reserves, owner's equity, cash, sales, and inventory.

Every business must keep track of the transactions which keep the company operating. This is the responsibility of the book-keeper, who, as the title suggests, keeps the "books." When someone speaks of a company's "books," he is referring to the journals and ledgers in which all financial information is re-corded. Paramount among these books is the general ledger, which is a summary of all the company's accounts and transactions.

Although approximately 90 percent of the nearly two million bookkeeping workers are women, men interested in pursuing a bookkeeping career should not be discouraged. Bookkeeping offers an excellent opportunity for both men and women who wish to enter and move up in the business world. More and more companies today rely heavily on their accounting and bookkeeping staffs to supply the personnel for management positions.

At entry level, an **assistant bookkeeper** may be assigned to a particular function such as accounts payable or receivable, or to a specific routine task such as checking invoices or billing. Naturally, however, an assistant bookkeeper needn't remain at that level; mastery of the basic skills will allow the bookkeeper in a large company to move up to a supervisory position or to move to a smaller company where he can assume the duties of a **general** or **full charge bookkeeper.**

WHAT DOES A BOOKKEEPER DO?

Regardless of its size, every business keeps a set of books. These books are a record of all assets, liabilities, and transactions. Without such a record, there would be virtually no way of knowing who owed the company money, to whom money was owed, how much stock was on hand, or what material had come in. In fact, none of the things which keep a company operating efficiently, and for which a company is operated, would be readily known or easily discoverable.

Depending upon its size, a company may have one full charge bookkeeper to handle all financial record-keeping or it may have an army of bookkeepers, supervisors, and assistants, each performing or responsible for a specific function or task.

Full Charge Bookkeeper

It is the responsibility of the full charge bookkeeper to analyze and record all of the company's financial transactions. Separate journals are usually employed for this. The **accounts receivable** journal is used to record billing and all money due the company; the **accounts payable** journal is a record of all money the company must pay. At the end of each week or month, the entries in the individual function journals are transferred to the **general ledger;** in this way, the company has a current, readily available summary of its financial position. In addition to making these entries, the full charge bookkeeper must check money taken in against money paid out to make sure that accounts "balance."

Posting the cash disbursement ledger

The full charge bookkeeper may also make out and mail the company's bills, calculate the payroll (including the deductions to be taken from each employee's wages), prepare checks, confirm invoices, and follow up unpaid bills. Because of the variety of the full charge bookeeper's duties, the opportunity for learning is much greater; however, since the responsibilities are also much greater, it is a more demanding job, requiring more time and, possibly, more dedication than a position in a large company.

A bookkeeping position in a large organization often involves one specific area. After a time, the bookkeeper may become a specialist in that area, and it is possible for him or her to rise to **head bookkeeper** and beyond—an opportunity not afforded to the full charge bookkeeper in a small company. Some large companies use complex bookkeeping machines to perform many of the routine duties; one advantage of working for an organization utilizing such machines is the opportunity to learn their operation, making the bookkeeper more valuable to that company and to future employers.

Assistant Bookkeeper

Assistant bookkeepers are responsible for many of the routine duties. This is often the entry-level position in the bookkeeping department of a large company. Until he has proven his proficiency and been promoted, the assistant bookkeeper will deal with the everyday details of recording payroll deductions and paid and due bills, as well as typing invoices, vouchers, and other financial records.

SKILL/PERSONALITY CHECKLIST

The following questions are designed to help you evaluate whether or not your abilities and personality indicate an aptitude for a position in bookkeeping. This is not, however, the last word; you should merely regard the result as an indication of your *present* status in relation to this position. This is not a test which you will either pass or fail. Answer the questions honestly, as your answers will help you determine the most suitable course for your future.

Respond to the questions in the following manner: **1** = little or no skill; **2** = moderate skill; **3** = superior skill. The questions relating to personality cannot, of course, be answered on the basis of skill; respond to these, numerically, as the others, on the basis of degree (1 = little or none; 2 = moderate; 3 = superior).

A total of between **14** and **23** indicates little or no aptitude for bookkeeping work; **24-33**, moderate aptitude; **34-42**, superior aptitude.

☐ Do you enjoy working with numbers?

☐ How proficient are you in all areas of arithmetic (adding, subtracting, multiplying, dividing)?

☐ How quickly can you add a column of figures?

☐ Are you an introspective (as opposed to an outgoing) person?

☐ How proficient are you in English (verbal and written)?

☐ Do you prefer being in a position in which others make the major decisions?

☐ Can you type?

☐ Can you use an adding machine?

☐ Do you know how to file?

☐ Do you know how to use a multiple-line telephone?

☐ How much do you know about the financial end of running a business?

☐ Do you enjoy working indoors?

☐ Do you prefer working by yourself?

☐ Are you attentive to detail?

SKILLS AND PERSONALITY

The preceding questions should have given you some basic ideas about the skills and interests preferable when planning to enter the field of bookkeeping. The first question suggests a primary requirement: you must enjoy working with numbers; and, as it usually follows that a person does well in something he likes to do, if you do enjoy working with numbers, you probably are good at it. The second requirement is fully as important as the first: the first ensures that you will enjoy your work; the second, that you will do your job well.

Since bookkeeping is an office occupation, you must prefer indoor to outdoor work; and, because a bookkeeper spends most of the day sitting at a desk and working at a set of books, it is preferable that you enjoy working alone (a certain amount of introspectiveness is also an asset).

Attention to detail is another necessity. Bookkeeping is all detail; a forgotten number or misplaced decimal point can have serious consequences. Attention to detail is a difficult quality to measure. Think about it carefully. Looking over work you have done recently might help you decide if this is an area which requires a concentrated effort at improvement.

Although bookkeeping does not require grammatical perfection or poetic phrasing, you will have to communicate in both verbal and written form; to avoid misunderstandings, you must be able to do so clearly.

A bookkeeper, even one in a supervisory position, is rarely called upon to make major decisions. To be content in your job, it is best if you are the type of person who does not crave authority, a person who prefers to do his best and leave major decisions to someone else. This is another area to which you should give considerable thought. Not everyone has either the desire or the aptitude for decision-making, and there is nothing wrong in this. If such a disinclination is part of your personality, it is far better to recognize it than to strive after a position of authority merely because you think it is expected of you. Doing your best in a job which suits you is really much more important than impressing others with authority which will only create problems for you.

As far as typing, using an adding machine, filing, and using a multiple-line telephone are concerned, these are acquired skills and a definite "plus" when applying for a job. If you presently have a basic familiarity with any or all of them, now is the time to perfect your skills; similarly, if you are unfamiliar with any or all of them, now is the time to learn. Knowledge of any business machine will be one more thing in your favor, regardless of which facet of the business world you enter.

It is difficult to learn about the financial end of running a business without being actively involved in it; but you can begin. Most high schools offer classes in business arithmetic, bookkeeping, and basic accounting. If yours does not, or if these classes are outside of your chosen curriculum, night classes and business schools can make up for the deficiency. If you have friends or relatives who are engaged in business, question them, ask them to explain their bookkeeping procedures to you. Probably the best way to learn is to begin working now. A part-time bookkeeping job will not only allow you to gain knowledge and experience not available in the classroom, but will give you that much of an edge when you apply for a full-time job.

One thing which you should not be concerned about at this time is the theory behind bookkeeping operations. Learn the "how." The "why" is important only if you plan to continue your education toward an accounting degree.

WHAT ARE THE OPPORTUNITIES?

As stated earlier, even entry-level bookkeeping positions can open up many excellent opportunities. If you specialize, you may rise, within that area, to supervisor or department head. A broader base will, of course, open a wider field for advancement; but this requires more than a high school education.

Unless you plan to go on to accounting, a bachelor's degree is not really necessary; an associate in arts degree, or even classes at a recognized business school, will make you considerably more valuable to your employer, and thus a much more appealing candidate for promotion.

Currently, a person looking for a bookkeeping position may virtually choose the industry he wishes to enter. Bookkeepers are needed in every kind of firm and in every area of business; wholesale and retail business use an especially large number (one-third of all bookkeepers presently employed work in one or the other of these areas). Other types of businesses using bookkeepers include banks, insurance companies, factories, publishing and communications firms, hospitals, and schools.

The number of jobs for bookkeepers is not expected to decrease; on the contrary, thousands of bookkeeping positions are expected to open up every year through 1985.

Many firms are turning more and more toward the use of bookkeeping machines and electronic data processing equipment. (It is, again, an added advantage if you know how to operate—or even have a general knowledge of—one or more such units.) These machines are designed to take over many of the more routine tasks, thus freeing the bookkeeper's time for those things which require human judgment. Electronic equipment is able to perform much faster, at lower cost, and—because a machine becomes neither tired, distracted, nor bored—often with greater accuracy than its human counterpart. However, even given the increasing use of these machines, the need for competent bookkeepers is expected to grow fast enough to cause these devices to have relatively little impact on the job market over the next five to ten years.

GETTING A JOB AS A BOOKKEEPER

If your interest is bookkeeping, if you have the aptitude for it, and if you plan on pursuing bookkeeping as a career, begin now.

Although it is possible to find a bookkeeping job immediately after graduating from high school (with a diploma but neither experience nor training), these positions are extremely rare. Almost invariably, you are already expected to have certain skills: you should, of course, be able to add, subtract, multiply, and divide rapidly and accurately; you should be able to type at least 30 to 35 words per minute (WPM), preferably with no more than one mistake per minute; you should be able to operate a simple, ten-key adding machine; copiers (Xerox or other type) and multiple-line telephones should also not be outside of your experience; and your handwriting should be quite neat. A basic knowledge of ledgers, journals, and invoices is necessary for advancement in the business world; however, this is information which can be learned on the job or in night classes while working, and is not usually a requirement for a position as an assistant bookkeeper or an accounts payable or accounts receivable clerk, or for one of the other entry-level positions.

As in other jobs, you should be conscientious and neat in appearance, arrive on time in the morning and be ready to work. You should be willing to learn from others and from your own mistakes, and willing also to work overtime on occasion. Although most of the actual work will be done on an individual basis, you will depend to a large degree on other workers for information, so you must be able to get along with people and, in a sense, work as part of a team.

SALARY, BENEFITS, AND WORKING CONDITIONS

If you plan to work part-time as a beginning accounting clerk during your remaining years in school, you can expect to receive between $3.00 and $4.00 per hour, depending, of course, upon the company and your skills.

Full-time beginning accounting clerks are paid between $140 and $160 per week. As your skill and experience increase, your salary will as well. An experienced accounting clerk can expect to be paid between $165 and $185 per week.

Benefits vary from company to company and should be considered before you accept employment. Many firms offer pension plans, profit sharing plans, payroll savings plans, major medical coverage, and other forms of insurance.

Most companies work a 40-hour week, except in the Northeast, where the standard work week is 35 hours. In most cases,

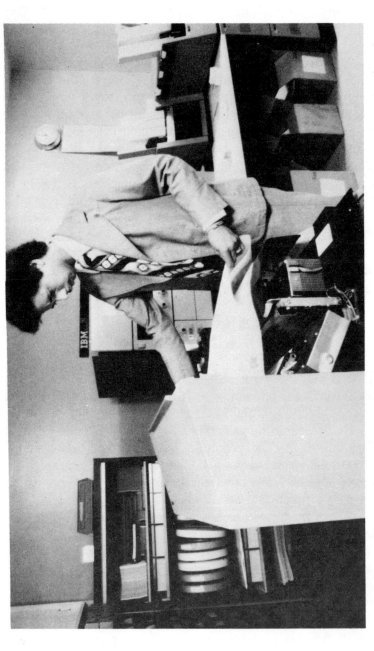

Many firms are turning to the use of electronic data processing equipment to provide bookkeeping functions.

workers receive seven or more paid holidays per year, a specified number of "sick days," and two weeks' paid vacation after having worked for one year. Longer vacations, usually based on the length of employment, may range up to four weeks or more.

3 The CASHIER

Cashiers receive money, make change, fill out charge forms, and give receipts.

Every business in which cash is taken in on a regular basis requires the services of a cashier. Such businesses include supermarkets, movie theaters, restaurants, and department stores. In some of these establishments, the cashier may be required to do more than just fulfill the functions of a cashier. In supermarkets, for example, the cashier, or checkout clerk, may have to wrap or bag purchases and, during slow periods, restock shelves. Cashiers in department stores may work part of the time as sales people. Ticket sellers in a theater may also answer telephone inquiries and work at the candy counter. Restaurant cashiers often take reservations, make arrangements for special parties, and sell whatever items are available at the cashier's counter. Many offices have cashiers. These, known as **agency** or **front office** cashiers, may also act as receptionists, do some typing and bookkeeping, and operate the switchboard.

Although businesses with a small cash flow may use nothing more than a cash drawer, most cashiers operate cash registers. Cash registers print the amount of the sale, and of each item, on a paper tape. If the machine does not do it automatically, the cashier must be able to compute the tax on the total of the sale or on the total of taxable items. Many businesses now use point-of-sale registers. These machines not only record the amount of sale and compute the tax, but they also record inventory numbers and other such information which is necessary for the reordering of merchandise. In fact, in some stores, the registers are connected to a computer which logs the sale of the particular item and indicates that it should be reordered when the stock has fallen to a certain level.

As you have probably noticed, many products and product labels are now printed with lines and numbers off to one side. This is called the UPC (universal product code). Eventually, stores (most notably supermarkets) will be equipped with registers which will automatically scan this code and record the price of the item. This will, of course, limit to some degree the number of trained cashiers needed in business generally. However, as full takeover of these fully automated registers is not expected to occur for some time, their use does not affect the immediate employment outlook.

SKILLS AND PERSONALITY

Although many companies offer on-the-job training for beginning cashiers, coming to the job with certain skills is beneficial.

If you are planning to become a cashier, you will find that courses in business arithmetic, typing, bookkeeping, and other business subjects will serve as good preparation. Cashier training, as a separate field, is offered as a part of many public school vocational programs. There are, in addition, a number of private cashier training schools. However, because of the cost involved, it is best to get as much training as possible through public programs and the rest through on-the-job training.

In large operations such as department stores and supermarkets, the use of cash registers and point-of-sale registers is part of on-the-job training. Smaller businesses usually prefer to hire persons who already have some experience in the operation of the machines used. If typing and/or using an adding machine is a part of the position, the employer will usually hire someone who is proficient in these areas.

If selling is a part of the position, the employer will generally hire someone who has the type of personality which lends itself to this kind of work. Such a person should not only be neat and personable (a requirement for any job in which one is dealing with the public), but should also be friendly and willing to help.

Most employers prefer someone with a high school diploma, although some are willing to hire high school students on a part-time basis.

Cashiers must be able to make change rapidly and accurately, perform repetitious tasks with no loss of accuracy, have a high degree of finger dexterity and eye-hand coordination, and be able to work accurately with figures.

Since many cashiers spend much of the working day on their feet, people planning on a job in this field should be able to do so without undue stress.

WHAT ARE THE OPPORTUNITIES?

Although jobs for cashiers are expected to increase approximately as fast as the average for all occupations through 1985, there may be a leveling-off or, possibly, a slump once the use of UPC registers becomes widespread.

Opportunities for advancement are somewhat limited for cashiers. However, as the job allows the cashier to learn about the particular business by which he or she is employed and about business in general, the job may lead to a better position in a field not directly related to cashiering. A cashier in a supermarket, for example, may be promoted to assistant manager or manager of the store. If the supermarket is part of a chain, as most are, the cashier may eventually be promoted to a position within the management of the company itself. A cashier in any other chain store may find similar opportunities: beginning as a cashier, being promoted to department manager and from there to buyer or store manager.

SALARY, BENEFITS, AND WORKING CONDITIONS

Beginning cashiers in non-union shops generally earn the current minimum wage. Experienced and/or unionized cashiers, many of whom work in supermarkets, earn between $3.50 and $5.75 per hour.

Part-time cashiers rarely receive any benefits beyond the opportunity to advance to a full-time position. In non-union shops, the benefits for full-time cashiers usually include a certain number of paid holidays and sick days, paid vacations based on the length of employment, and may include medical insurance and a pension plan. Unionized cashiers receive all of the above mentioned benefits, as negotiated in the current union contract.

Most cashiers stand for most of the workday. In addition, because check-out counters are often near the door, many cashiers are subject to drafts, the summer's heat, and the winter's cold. Cashiers are also generally required to work on Saturday (and sometimes on Sunday), although they are given other days off during the week. In the case of cashiers who work in restaurants and movie theaters, the job usually entails working at night and possibly on a split-shift schedule.

4 The CLERK

File, Stock, Shipping & Receiving, Statistical

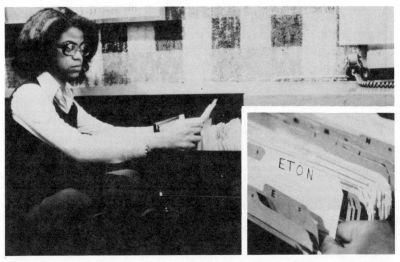

Clerks keep records and accounts and perform routine office tasks.

Clerks constitute the single largest group of office workers. There are approximately ten times as many clerks as there are bookkeepers and five times as many as there are stenographers. These ratios are likely to change in the future as machines take over many of the duties currently performed by clerks, but there will still be a considerable number of clerks needed in business, especially clerks who are able to operate the new equipment.

There are a number of different kinds of clerks (such as general clerk, file clerk, stock clerk, shipping and receiving clerk and statistical clerk), and although their duties are generally of a similar nature, the individual tasks vary from one position to another.

Clerks are at the lower end of the office occupations ladder, and the position carries with it some initial disadvantages. Salary is one disadvantage. Because the job does not require extensive education or unusual skills, the salary is often low. Two other disadvantages are monotony and pressure. A clerk's job consists mainly of routine work which can soon become monotonous. Pressure, the final disadvantage, may occur during those peak work periods during which there is a great deal of paper work to be done. This pressure may be increased if, as is the case in some companies, a standard is set (not unlike factory piecework) for the amount of work to be done in a specified time.

The major advantage in this field is the fact that clerks' jobs are fairly plentiful and, if one is willing to endure the initial disadvantages, they offer a good opportunity for entering a company or an area of expertise and later moving to more responsible and financially rewarding positions.

WHAT DOES A CLERK DO?

General Clerk

The duties of a general clerk are varied and may include some of the following.

- Typing (letters, numerical data, reports, printed forms)

- Typing from recordings and operating the recording machine

- Doing research

- Recording data (in typed or handwritten form)

- Duplicating (on Xerox—or similar machine—or offset press)

- Proofreading

- Checking figures

- Sorting and storing documents

- Cataloging data

- Using an adding or calculating machine

- Retrieving needed documents or information

Naturally, a clerk's duties may not include all of the listed tasks. On the other hand, however, his duties may indeed include all of these plus others related to the specific function in which he is engaged.

File Clerk

In order for a company to operate efficiently, information and documents must be stored in such a way that needed data are readily available and incoming data are able to be stored quickly and properly. Such a filing system must be maintained, and it is the file clerk who is responsible for keeping the records accurate, up to date, and properly placed.

When information is needed, the file clerk must locate it, log it out, and correctly replace it when returned.

When a piece of information comes into the office, the file clerk reads it and, based on the system used by that company for filing, puts it in its proper place. Later, when that information is requested, the file clerk retrieves it. In addition, the file clerk must keep track of what materials are borrowed and see to it that they are returned.

Some offices use mechanized, rotating files. The file clerk must be able to operate this equipment. Some offices use microfilm for recording information. When a piece of information is requested, the file clerk must locate the microfilm strip containing the information and put it on an electronic transmitter which displays the information on a screen.

Unless files are kept up to date, they become cluttered with material which is no longer in use. Thus the file clerk may periodically destroy the out-of-date information or transfer it to a storage area where non-current records are kept.

In a large organization, the file clerk may do nothing but work with the files. In a small office, however, the file clerk may be called upon to perform some of the duties listed under general clerk.

Stock Clerk

If a company deals in goods, it must maintain a well balanced inventory. If it does not, it may find that goods in demand are not available in its warehouse and that the warehouse is over-stocked with items not in demand. The same situation is true of manufacturing companies. If an item is needed to keep the production line going and is unavailable, a slowdown in production results, causing a loss of sales.

It is the function of the stock clerk to prevent such situations. He must control the flow of material received, stored, and issued.

When goods arrive, the stock clerk usually unpacks, checks the merchandise, and records it, thus keeping a constant tally of the quantity available in stock. Before goods are shipped, the stock clerk checks the order to make sure that the proper quantity is being shipped and that the material is in good condition. The stock clerk may also be called upon to make minor repairs or adjustments if something is wrong with the merchandise. It is also part of the stock clerk's job to report (and process whatever papers are necessary) any damaged or spoiled merchandise.

Just as files are arranged according to a specified system, merchandise must be arranged in such a way that an item may be easily stored and easily located. When goods arrive, the stock clerk usually marks the items with a code or a price and then stores it in its proper place.

The stock clerk takes an inventory to assure that merchandise levels are adequate.

A stock clerk may also be responsible for packing and addressing merchandise for delivery. He may, in addition, if the company is a relatively small one, assume the duties of shipping and receiving clerk.

Shipping and Receiving Clerk

In a small company, one clerk may take care of all shipping and receiving. In a large company, however, each function may be handled by one clerk or several clerks.

Shipping and receiving clerks keep track of all merchandise sent to the company by its suppliers and all goods which the company sends to its customers.

The **receiving** clerk is responsible for all goods arriving at the company. He checks the incoming material against the original order and the invoice or bill of lading which accompanies the shipment. The quantity and condition of the material is then recorded. If any of the goods have been lost or damaged during transport, the receiving clerk must make whatever adjustments with the shippers are required. Plotting the movement of goods within the organization, as well as providing the information needed to keep inventories at their proper levels, may also be part of the receiving clerk's job.

The **shipping** clerk is responsible for all merchandise sent from a company to its customers. He checks all orders before they go out to make sure that the proper quantity, in good condition, is being sent. Because the shipping clerk is responsible for sending material, he must have a knowledge of postal and private company shipping rates. After a shipment is packed, the shipping clerk weighs and records the weight and shipping cost of each parcel. He then moves the shipment to the loading area and oversees the loading operation, directing the loading of each parcel according to its destination.

It may also be part of the shipping clerk's job to prepare invoices and supply information about shipments to other departments in the company.

Statistical Clerk

Statistical clerk is a general designation for someone whose job involves preparing and ensuring the accuracy of numerical records. This designation may be divided into four categories (each of which may be further divided into areas of specialization):

1. Recording

2. Compiling and coding

3. Computing and tabulating

4. Scheduling

Recording involves collecting information and verifying its accuracy. Shipping checkers make sure that merchandise to be shipped is properly labeled and addressed and contains the correct quantity. **Counters** (whose complete title may include the items they count or the work in which they are involved) record the number of items produced, received, or transferred.

Compiling and coding deals with information which must be filed, verified, or analyzed by computer. Posting clerks are responsible for providing company officials with information on current business activities. To do this, they sort records of production, shipments, and financial transactions and enter this information in journals and registers. Coding clerks code information for transfer to computer cards.

Statistical clerks involved in **computing and tabulating** gather numerical information from records to present in a chart or table for analysis. Policy checkers verify insurance company records. Actuary clerks prepare graphs and charts on general insurance practices and assist actuaries in determining the risk involved in providing insurance coverage. Statistical assistants (or tabulating clerks) calculate and compute numerical data for research projects.

In many businesses, the movement of personnel and equipment is crucial to efficient operation. Statistical clerks are in-

Statistical clerks are responsible for the accuracy of minute but important data.

volved in much of this **scheduling.** They may, for example (as crew schedulers for airlines or bus companies), assign pilots or drivers to a particular flight or run and keep track of the mileage accumulated. Or, as in the case of a gas dispatcher, they may consider all the conditions which affect the flow and use of natural gas to determine the proper pressure in the gas-line to meet customers' needs.

SKILLS AND PERSONALITY

The clerk, as a part of the overall operation of a business, must be aware of the responsibility of the position he or she holds. The functions performed by the clerk are necessary to the organization. The clerk must not feel that he or she is a mere functionary, for if that is the point of view, he or she will be unable to exercise judgment and initiative when they are required. Further, the clerk, especially if he or she has never before worked in an actual business situation, must recognize the necessity for accuracy, promptness, neatness, and meeting deadlines.

Most companies require that all clerks have at least a high school diploma. Since on-the-job training is costly, most firms also prefer that clerks have some training in clerical skills. Many high schools have curricula specifically designed to train students for clerical positions. The courses usually included are: typing, bookkeeping, an introductory course in business economics, and general office procedures. Many high schools also offer classes in data processing. As more and more clerical tasks are assumed by the computer, businesses look more and more for clerks who understand, at least, the basic concepts of data processing.

Additional skills a clerk should have include:

- Ability to listen and carry out instructions

- Reading

- Basic mathematics (and more specifically, business math and some bookkeeping)

- Ability to write clearly, observing the rules of grammar, spelling, punctuation, and sentence construction

- Ability to use an adding machine and ten-key calculator

If the position involves making entries, by hand, in journals or registers, neat handwriting is also sought. (However, neat, legible handwriting is always an asset, regardless of the specific tasks involved in a job.)

Four standards which have been established for an entry-level clerical position are:

1. The ability to type at least forty words per minute with no more than one error per minute

2. The ability to insert or remove file cards at the rate of 300 per hour

3. The ability to cut a mimeograph stencil in twenty minutes

4. The ability to type an average of 125 addresses (on envelopes or form letters) per hour

As technology becomes a greater part of office operations, the clerk will have to be able to respond not only to these new methods of collecting, processing, sorting, and retrieving information, but also to the new environment which these methods will create in offices.

WHAT ARE THE OPPORTUNITIES?

As more companies begin using computers to handle many of the routine tasks presently handled by clerks, the number of openings will decrease to some extent. However, new jobs will open up for those who have prepared for this and acquired some training in the new methods.

Employment opportunities for **general clerks** and **file clerks** will have to keep pace with the growing volume of paper work. However, as noted, this pace will be slowed somewhat as computers are used more extensively to arrange, store, and transmit information. Many employers currently use part-time clerks during peak business periods; and, since computers must be operated on a 24 hour-per-day basis for their use to be economically viable, additional opportunities will be available for part-time, swing-shift, and night-shift work for those clerks who possess the necessary skills.

Again, the increase in the number of **stock clerks** necessary will be slowed by the use of computers for inventory control. Also, because entrance into this position has traditionally been relatively easy, thus prompting many recent high school graduates to apply for it as their first job, some competition may be encountered.

The technology which affects other clerks' jobs will also affect the positions available for **shipping and receiving clerks.** Although it is expected that the amount of merchandise to be moved will increase, the number of shipping and receiving clerks needed to move the goods will be fewer than would have been required in the past. Once again, a basic knowledge of computer technology will be an asset in finding and holding a position as a shipping and receiving clerk.

The **statistical clerk** may be the position most affected by the advances in computer science. Since statistical clerks, regardless of the particular specialization involved, deal primarily with numbers, and because computers are able to perform the same operations much more rapidly and accurately, the number of statistical clerks needed in business will not increase much.

Opportunities for promotion from the position of clerk are fairly good; better, at the present time, for men than women, as men tend to be promoted more rapidly. Unless a clerk specializes in one area, he or she deals with many facets of the company's business. Thus, there is a broad range of opportunities for advancement. A clerk having some stenographic training may move from clerk to stenographer to secretary. Another may be promoted to assistant supervisor of the clerical pool, and from there to supervisor. It is also possible for a clerk to move into an area of employment totally unrelated to the position for which he or she was originally hired. For example, a clerk who finds that he or she has a preference for selling might move into the sales department; similarly, another might find personnel work appealing and move in that direction.

The opportunities outlined above also exist for those clerks who go into specialized areas (file, stock, etc.), although to a somewhat lesser degree of diversity, since he or she comes into contact with fewer general office procedures and fewer people outside his or her particular department.

Many offices periodically rate employees to determine their current standing and readiness for promotion. The qualities most supervisors look for and evaluate are:

- Proficiency in one's present position and knowledge of those related to it

- Neatness and accuracy

- How much work one does and how quickly a particular task is completed

- Initiative, as well as the ability to follow instructions

- Relations with co-workers

- The ability to learn and adapt to new methods and techniques

GETTING A JOB AS A CLERK

There are a number of avenues available to the person seeking a position as a clerk: want ads in newspapers, the state employment office, a private employment agency, and school placement offices (whether high school, vocational school, or private business school). Any one of these should provide the job seeker with a number of openings for which to apply. Most private employment agencies charge a fee for their services, and this fee may range anywhere from a week's to a month's salary which, if the employee is responsible for paying it, may be paid off in installments. In some cases, of course, the employer pays the fee, but this is not usually true of entry-level positions.

Aside from the skills mentioned earlier, employers look for employees who are willing to take their job seriously and recognize their place in the overall operation of the company. Neatness and courtesy are both considered by most employers to be indications of a serious-minded attitude and a recognition that business is business.

If you plan on applying for a clerical position after graduation from high school, taking the *National Business Entrance Tests* before graduation will help you get that first job. The tests cover six areas: 1) Business Fundamentals and General Information, 2) Machine Calculation, 3) Typewriting, 4) Stenography, 5) General Office Clerical, and 6) Bookkeeping and Accounting. The certificate given upon passing these tests almost invariably increases the chance of finding a job.

SALARY, BENEFITS, AND WORKING CONDITIONS

The average salary for entry-level general clerks, file clerks, and statistical clerks is $110 per week. The average salary for beginning stock clerks and shipping and receiving clerks is about $120 per week.

As in most other office occupations, the benefits include between seven and ten paid holidays per year, paid vacations (whose length depends upon the length of employment), hospitalization insurance, sick days, and pension plans. Some companies may offer an education program.

Working conditions for general clerks, file clerks, and statistical clerks are the same as for most other office occupations.

Working conditions for stock clerks and shipping and receiving clerks, however, may vary considerably.

Stock clerks usually work in fairly clean, heated, and well-lighted areas. This, however, is not always the case. Some stockrooms may be damp and drafty, and stock clerks handling refrigerated merchandise may spend part of the day in cold storage rooms. Stock clerks also spend much of the day on their feet, often on a concrete floor. The job may also entail considerable bending, lifting, and climbing.

Although shipping and receiving clerks spend much of the time in the warehouse or the shipping and receiving rooms, they may also be required to spend hours outside on the loading dock while merchandise is being loaded or unloaded. The warehouse itself is often a large, unpartitioned area which is not always adequately lighted or heated. Shipping and receiving clerks also stand for long periods checking merchandise or overseeing loading or unloading operations. As with the stock clerk, the shipping and receiving clerk may also have to do a considerable amount of bending, lifting, and climbing; in fact, a shipping and receiving clerk may have to do more of this than a stock clerk, especially during those times when, under pressure of getting shipments moved on time, he helps to load or unload merchandise.

5 The COLLECTION WORKER

Collection workers contact debtors by mail and telephone to convince them to pay their overdue bills.

"Buy now, pay later" is a phrase with which most of us are familiar, and although it has become something of a cliché, it does, quite accurately, state the way much business in the United States is transacted. Credit (credit cards, loans, checking account overdraft protection, charge accounts) has become *the* way of life for many individuals and many companies.

When it happens that an individual or a company is unable to pay a debt, the creditor may "turn the bill over for collection." If the creditor is a bank, loan company, large store, or other company which has its own collection department, this entails sending all pertinent information to the head of that department who, in turn, gives the account to a member of his staff. Individuals, smaller companies, and even large companies which either don't have a collection department or, for some reason, have decided to seek outside assistance, generally turn their uncollected debts over to a professional collection agency. Collection agencies make money by charging a percentage of the amount collected from the debtor.

Collection workers (also called **bill collectors** or **collection correspondents**) employed by collection agencies work at various levels. At the retail level, the point at which most collection workers begin, the worker is engaged primarily with smaller debts, usually incurred by customers of stores and other small businesses. The collection workers handling such cases most often deal directly with the principals involved: the business and the individual debtor.

At the corporate level (the province of experienced workers), the collection correspondent may have to deal with corporate officers and attorneys representing both parties involved.

WHAT DOES A
COLLECTION WORKER DO?

When normal billing methods, such as monthly statements or form letters, fail to elicit payment, the account is often turned over to a collection agency or to the collection department.

Once in the hands of the agency or department, a bad debt file is made. This file, which may be compiled either by a clerk or the collection worker, contains all information pertinent to the case: information about the debtor, the nature of the debt, the amount still outstanding, and the date of the last payment. The collector then contacts the debtor by mail, telephone, or both. If this initial contact is made by mail, the letter is very often done by a system (computer, automatic typewriter, or multiple-part form). The collection worker must be familiar with the systems used in order to monitor them.

The collection worker usually tries to find out the reason that the bill has not been paid. To do this, the debtor is most often contacted by telephone.

Non-payment of a bill can result from a number of causes, and the cause usually determines the approach a collector will take with a particular case. A customer may feel that he is being cheated in some way: the bill is incorrect, the services for which he contracted were not done properly, the merchandise purchased was faulty. If this is the case, and if the bill is being handled by a collection agency, the collector usually recommends that the debtor contact the original seller and attempt to resolve the disputed bill. If collection is being done through the collection department of the store itself, the collection worker will probably turn the account over to the "customer service" department, which is set up in most large stores to deal with this kind of problem. This having been done, if the bill is still not paid, the collector will again contact the debtor and attempt to convince him that he was billed correctly and should pay the debt.

If the debt is the result of a loan, credit card account, or other instance in which money was advanced, the collection worker may arrange to have the loan refinanced or arrange a new payment schedule which meets with the debtor's budget.

If the debt has been incurred by a major purchase (automobile, refrigerator, etc.), the collection worker may arrange to have a new loan issued for payment of the bill, or the collector may, again, arrange a new payment schedule which better suits the debtor's financial position.

All of these proceedings are generally done by mail and telephone. If the debt is a fairly large one, however, and if the collector has failed to convince the debtor to pay his bill, a personal call may become necessary.

Whether the debtor is contacted by telephone or in person, however, the collection worker often acts as a financial advisor. The collector may find that the debtor has not met his obligation because of an unexpected financial emergency. Such an emergency may be loss of employment, sudden illness in the family, an accident, or house repairs which had to be made for the reasons of health or safety. Non-payment of a bill may also be caused by mismanagement of funds or overextension (contracting for more goods and services than one can pay for). When such a situation is encountered, the collection worker often helps the debtor arrange some means of paying the bills with the money and income he does have.

When all methods of trying to convince the debtor to pay his debt have failed, the collection worker may, unless the creditor has decided to "write off" the bad debt, turn the case over to an attorney for legal action against the debtor. If the case involves merchandise which is to be repossessed, the collection worker may supervise the repossession proceedings.

If a debtor has moved without leaving a forwarding address, the collection worker may be called upon to locate him. In large collection agencies, this work is often done by specialized collection workers known as **tracers.** The process of finding a debtor who has moved is usually done by following the leads obtained at the post office; through the debtor's friends, former neighbors, and places of employment; by searching telephone directories, and by following trails such as the issuance of a driver's license or automobile registration.

If the collection agency is a relatively small one, the collection worker may have duties besides contacting debtors. The collector may act as financial advisor to customers (creditors) of the collection agency who may be having financial difficulties. In addition, the collection worker may periodically contact customers to find out if they are satisfied with the job the collection agency is doing.

The collection correspondent working at the corporate level is usually involved in more personal contact with the parties. Since such cases usually involve large sums of money, often tens or even hundreds of thousands of dollars, the collection agency generally feels that spending the amount of time necessary to pursue the case in this manner is justifiable.

SKILL/PERSONALITY CHECKLIST

The following questions are designed to help you evaluate whether or not your abilities and personality indicate an aptitude for a position as a collection worker. This is not, however, the last word; you should merely regard the result as an indication of your *present* status in relation to this position. This is not a test which you will either pass or fail. Answer the questions honestly, as your answers will help you determine the most suitable course for your future.

Respond to the questions in the following manner: **1** = little or no skill; **2** = moderate skill; **3** = superior skill. The questions relating to personality cannot, of course, be answered on the basis of skill; respond to them numerically, as the others, on the basis of degree (**1** = little or none; **2** = moderate; **3** = superior).

☐ How persuasive do you consider yourself?

☐ How well can you communicate (verbal and written language skills)?

☐ How tenacious are you?

☐ Are you able to get along with different people?

☐ How well do you handle yourself in difficult situations (include alertness, imagination and quickness of wit)?

☐ Are you sympathetic when confronted with other people's problems?

☐ Do you have a pleasant telephone manner and speaking voice?

☐ Can you type?

☐ How familiar are you with data processing equipment and automatic typewriters?

☐ Do you have any knowledge of basic office procedures?

☐ Are you familiar with the use of common office machines (adding machines, calculators, copiers)?

If you wish to rate your aptitude for collection work, score the preceding checklist as follows:
11 to **18** — Little or no aptitude
19 to **25** — Moderate aptitude
26 to **33** — Superior aptitude

SKILLS AND PERSONALITY

The person who succeeds as a collection worker is usually **persuasive** rather than aggressive. The common idea of the bill collector beating down the door is largely a misconception. Not only do most reputable collection agencies neither expect nor condone such behavior, the government's consumer protection agencies have strictly forbidden it. Persuasion must be calm and logical; a process of convincing, not threatening. In dealing with most people, but especially those you are trying to convince to pay their debts, aggression will usually serve only to turn them against you. Since the primary function of a collection worker is to collect the money due the collection agency's clients, hostility is the worst possible attitude you can create in a debtor.

Language is the collection worker's basic tool. In order to convince a debtor to pay the money he owes, you must be able to communicate well in both verbal and written form.

Tenacity, the ability to stay with something to its conclusion, is one of the most important traits of a successful collection worker. A collection case often drags on for months, requiring the collection worker to make repeated calls on the debtor, to write numerous letters, and to say, virtually, the same thing over and over again. Such a situation can become discouraging. Unless you have the tenacity to stay with the case to the end, you will not frequently succeed in collecting the money owed the agency's client.

As a collection worker, you will come into contact with a great variety of people, and you must be able to get along with all of them. If you yourself are difficult to get along with, it is unlikely that you will be able to win the confidence of, and thus persuade, those people who have not paid an outstanding bill.

Just as you will come into contact with a great variety of people, you will also, as a collection worker, encounter many different and often difficult situations. Most people dislike being reminded that they owe money which they have failed to pay. Reactions to being asked to pay will vary with each individual, and you must be able **to cope** with difficult situations.

The question of sympathy is a difficult one. You must be **sympathetic**; if you are not, you will be unable to appreciate the plight of the debtor, you will not truly desire to help him, and thus help the collection agency's client, and you will probably arouse the debtor's antagonism. On the other hand, if you are too sympathetic, you may not be persuasive enough to convince the debtor to pay the money he owes.

As a collection worker, most of your work will be done by telephone. Because of this, **a pleasant voice and manner** are virtually indispensible.

As in most other office occupations, **typing** is an asset to the collection worker. If you cannot type but have the more important qualities outlined above, you are likely to obtain a position regardless; typing is merely one more thing in your favor.

The data processing equipment and automatic typewriters used by collection agencies are, at the collection worker's level of involvement with them, used primarily for composing form letters. After you have obtained a position as a collection worker, you will be taught as much as you need to know about these systems. However, if you can bring this knowledge with you to the job, it is likely to be an inducement to your being hired in preference to someone who is unfamiliar with this equipment.

Familiarity with basic office procedures and the use of common office machines is also a valuable, but not absolutely a necessary asset. You will be taught these things on the job, but if you already know something about them, your employer will be saved the time and expense of teaching you.

WHAT ARE THE OPPORTUNITIES?

Because of the image most people have of collection workers, many people have been reluctant to go into the field. The image is changing. The collection worker is now also seen in the role of debt counselor, and collection methods have been modified to conform to modern management practices and recent consumer legislation—and there are excellent employment opportunities.

The areas of greatest competition are collection agencies (because there are relatively few of them) and large metropolitan banks (because they generally offer higher salaries and better opportunities for advancement). The area offering the best opportunity for initial employment is the retail trade. As large stores extend credit to more and more people, the number of bad debts increases and so does the need for collection personnel.

Opportunities for advancement in the retail collection field are, however, somewhat limited. Competition for promotion is fairly keen and positions are fairly scarce; the collection worker with superior abilities may, however, become a collection manager or supervisor of the collection department.

In the larger collection agencies, opportunities for advancement are somewhat better. The collection worker may rise from the retail level to the corporate level. Beyond that is the sales department. At that level, the worker is no longer involved in the collection of debts, but is a representative for the collection agency, selling that company's services to other businesses.

Banks offer the greatest diversity of advancement opportunities. Once a position in the bank's collection department has been secured, one may move up in that area or move to a different area, such as the loan department.

GETTING A JOB AS
A COLLECTION WORKER

In most cases, a high school education is sufficient for getting a job as a collection worker. Employers are generally more interested in finding someone with the personality and abilities which fit the position than they are in hiring someone with an extensive educational background.

However, a certain direction in your high school education will make you a more appealing candidate for employment.

Naturally, business courses will be of value. Such courses might include bookkeeping, general office procedures, business math, typing, and stenography. Although these skills are not necessary for getting a job in the collection field, they will be assets which most employers will take into account. In addition, having these skills will make you more comfortable in an office environment.

As mentioned earlier, language skills are by far the most important to a collection worker, and, as an adjunct to this, speech classes can prove very useful. Since a collection worker deals with people on a person-to-person basis in a rather sensitive area, training in the basics of psychology can be quite helpful.

Previous employment as a sales clerk can also help. Employment in this area will give the collector an insight into the way in which credit transactions originate and how they are handled at the point of sale.

SALARY, BENEFITS, AND WORKING CONDITIONS

The average wage for a beginning collection worker in a collection agency which pays on a straight salary basis is about $150 per week. This figure may be slightly higher for a collector in a bank's collection department and slightly lower for a worker in the retail field.

Although many collection agencies pay their collectors a straight salary, many others do not. Instead, they pay on the basis of salary plus commission. Commission schedules vary greatly from one agency to another. A collection worker in one agency may be paid a relatively high salary and a low commission percentage. A collector in another agency may receive a fairly low salary and a rather high commission. Some agencies pay their collectors on a straight commission basis, but these agencies are few. As an added incentive to their collection personnel, some collection agencies assign a quota to a collector or group of collectors and pay a bonus if this quota is reached.

Benefits and working conditions are virtually the same in this industry as they are in other office occupations. The work is indoors, at a desk, and involves spending a good part of the work day speaking on the telephone.

Most collection workers receive between seven and eleven paid holidays per year, two-weeks vacation after one year's employment, a specified number of sick days, and health insurance. A collection worker who must make visits outside the office is either provided transportation by the company or reimbursed for the expenses involved in the trip.

6 HOTEL OFFICE PERSONNEL

Hotel and motel front office personnel welcome guests, provide information, handle room reservations, issue keys, collect payments, and bill guests. Hotel and motel managers and assistant managers determine room rates and credit policy, direct kitchen and dining room operations, and oversee the housekeeping, accounting, and maintenance departments.

There are tens of thousands of hotels in the United States, ranging in size from those with only a few rooms to those with more than 1,000 rooms. Some of these establishments provide no more than a comfortable place for travelers to spend the night, while others offer luxurious surroundings, fine restaurants and night clubs, and other amenities for their guests. In addition to hotels and motels, there are resorts. Many of these have existed for years, but with the increase in leisure time available to a large percentage of the population, many more resorts are being opened each year.

Regardless of the size and the services it offers, every hotel, motel, and resort has certain jobs which must be performed by office personnel. In the case of a small hotel or motel, all of these duties may fall to members of the owner's family. Large hotels, on the other hand, may have hundreds of employees and half-a-dozen managers.

Office positions in hotels and motels range from night clerk to general manager. There may also be bookkeepers, secretaries, accountants, and telephone operators. These jobs are fairly similar to the same positions in other fields. The positions of night clerk, desk (or room clerk), reservation clerk, rack clerk, front office manager, assistant manager, and general manager are, however, peculiar to the hotel/motel/resort industry.

Of course, not every hotel or motel needs a large staff. If a couple owns a small, roadside motel with fifteen or twenty units, it is more than likely that between them they will perform all the managerial, clerical, housekeeping, and groundskeeping duties. This, naturally, is not possible in a 1,000 room hotel. In such establishments, duties are divided much as they are in large corporations, with a general manager at the top, who, if the hotel is part of a chain, reports to the president or board of directors of the organization; a number of assistant managers, each of whom is responsible for one area of operations; and a corps of clerks to perform the routine duties of running the hotel.

WHAT DO HOTEL OFFICE PERSONNEL DO?

Because most hotels and motels run on a twenty-four hour per day basis, many services must be available at any time during the day or night. Most of a hotel's business and clerical work is, of course, done during normal working hours. However, regardless of the time of day or night, there must be someone at the front desk, there must be a telephone operator (if the hotel has a switchboard), and there must be a manager in attendance. Because hotels are usually not particularly busy at night, many beginning front desk personnel are put on the night shift. They are thereby able to learn the various operations without the pressure of daytime activity. These operations are, however, the same as those performed during the day; thus these positions and the duties they entail are usually equally applicable to day and night work.

Mail clerks, key clerks, information clerks, and floor clerks are separate positions only in the largest hotels and resorts. **Mail clerks** sort and distribute mail. **Key clerks** issue keys. **Information clerks** answer whatever questions guests may have regarding the hotel, its services, and the surrounding area. **Floor clerks** distribute mail, packages, and telegrams to the guests on that floor; they also act as watchmen, protecting the hotel from the intrusion of unauthorized persons.

Desk clerks assign rooms and answer questions about hotel policy, facilities, and services. The assignment of rooms must meet two criteria: it must satisfy the guest and it must maximize the hotel's revenue. Desk clerks also fill out registration cards or forms for guests and, if the hotel does not have a cashier or if the cashier is not on duty, the desk clerk may collect guests' payments.

Reservation clerks record requests for reservations. These requests may have arrived in the form of letters or telegrams, or they may have been telephoned. The reservation clerk must keep a written account of all reservation requests, complete the registration cards or forms, and notify the room clerk of the guests' arrival times, requests as to size or type of room, and any other specific instructions which may have been included in the reservation request.

Rack clerks keep records of room assignments. They are responsible for advising housekeepers, telephone operators, maintenance workers, and other hotel personnel that a room is occupied.

Hotel managers and assistant managers are responsible for maintaining the hotel's profitable operation. Front desk clerks are responsible for all of the routine, customer-related duties.

Hotel managers and **assistant managers** are responsible for maintaining the hotel's profitable operation and for satisfying guests' requests. Unless the hotel is part of a chain which has laid down regulations and specifications for all of its hotels, the manager sets room rates and determines the hotel's credit policy. If the hotel is a large one, offering a number of services and facilities beyond sleeping accommodations, the general manager usually has a number of assistants, each of whom is responsible for a particular area of operations.

If the hotel has banquet and/or convention facilities, there is generally an assistant manager in charge of these operations. His or her responsibilities include: reserving the time and, if the hotel has more than one meeting room, the particular one in which the event will take place; arranging for the proper amount and type of seating (that is, it may be just a meeting or it may be a dinner); setting up the speaker's platform; arranging the menu if a meal is to be served; and contracting for any additional help (waiters, waitresses, bartenders, etc.) which may be required.

A hotel's restaurant and cocktail lounge are generally quite profitable and therefore important to the overall success of the establishment. There are, of course, hotels in which these facilities are not run directly by the hotel. The space is merely rented from the hotel, and the hotel takes no part in the operation. If, however, the restaurant, lounge, and (in some hotels and resorts) night club are operated by the hotel, there is usually an assistant manager whose sole responsibility is the running of these rooms. In some cases, each room may have its own manager. More often, though, they are all under the charge of one individual, who, almost invariably, has had experience in the restaurant field.

Although the **housekeeper** may not actually be considered a manager, his or her duties are basically administrative. The executive, or head housekeeper is responsible for supervising the housekeeping staff, which may number from a dozen to several hundred workers. He or she also prepares the budget for the housekeeping department, suggests improvements in housekeeping procedure, reports to the general manager on the condition of rooms and needed repairs, and purchases supplies and furnishings. The executive housekeeper may have an assistant to help in the adminsitration of the department. He or she may also have a number of floor housekeepers, each of whom may be responsible for overseeing the cleaning and maintenance of one or several floors in the hotel.

Large hotels and resorts may also have **public relations** departments. The director of this department and his or her staff is, like the public relations department in a corporation, responsible for keeping a positive image of the hotel before the public. However, unlike its corporate counterpart, the hotel and resort public relations department may also be called upon to give special attention to VIP's, who may either be guests or performers in the hotel's entertainment facilities.

SKILLS AND PERSONALITY

The primary requirement for anyone wishing to work in a hotel is an aptitude for working well with the public. Included in this general characteristic are a courteous and friendly manner, a desire to help people, and a neat appearance.

A high school education is generally adequate for entry-level employment, but additional training is an asset in obtaining a promotion to the managerial level. Typing ability is helpful in all hotel office positions, as is the ability to operate an adding machine. Although operation of the posting machine used at the front desk of many hotels is generally taught on the job, a familiarity with the machine is likely to create a favorable impression when applying for a job. Finally, a knowledge of bookkeeping is helpful for work at the front desk of a small hotel.

Naturally, one doesn't walk into a hotel and get a job as a manager. However, one can prepare for eventual promotion to that position. Experience is still considered the hotel manager's most important attribute, but more and more hotels and hotel chains are stressing the educational aspect of managerial preparation. A four-year college course in hotel and restaurant administration is, of course, excellent training for a career in this field, and with such a degree, one might very well walk into a hotel and get a job as an assistant manager. Other training which is not only helpful, but is available to someone who is working, are courses in hotel work given at some junior colleges, those available through the American Hotel and Motel Association, and programs offered by private hotel training schools (of either the classroom or correspondence variety).

Managers must have self-discipline and initiative, as well as the ability to delegate responsibility and organize and direct the work of others. The manager of a small hotel may also have to do much of the front desk work; thus, he or she must have all the skills and attributes necessary in a front desk clerk.

In the field of housekeeping, most employers prefer to hire applicants who have graduated from high school. Beyond this, experience is considered the best teacher, with additional education running a strong second. Such additional education may be obtained at colleges and universities which offer programs of study in hotel and motel administration, including classes in housekeeping. These classes are often given at night, thus enabling the promotion-seeking housekeeper to obtain some additional education while working. In addition to these classes, many schools have developed programs under the approval and guidance of the National Executive Housekeepers Association. The American Hotel and Motel Association also offers housekeeping courses for classroom or home study.

Like managers, executive housekeepers must have self-discipline and initiative, as well as the ability to delegate responsibility and organize and direct the work of others. In addition, executive housekeepers should have a knowledge of budget preparation and interior decoration, and know the best methods involved in the purchase, use, and care of different types of equipment and fabrics.

WHAT ARE THE OPPORTUNITIES?

Generally, employment in the hotel and motel industry is expected to grow at a rate comparable to that of other industries during the next ten years. Although a large percentage of the jobs available will be front office positions, some setbacks may occur due to the increasing use of computer reservation systems by hotel and motel chains.

Opportunity for advancement once one has a job in a hotel or motel is fairly good. Although bellhops, elevator operators, and other non-office personnel are occasionally transferred to the front desk, this is the exception rather than the rule. Individuals who wish to get into office work in the hotel industry have a better chance of advancing if they begin in office jobs.

Entry-level employment is usually as a mail clerk, key clerk, or information clerk. Training is usually on the job. During the brief training period, the new employee is given information about the hotel and its services, and the duties of the position are explained. In addition, the newly hired worker is usually instructed in the operation of any machines which are part of the routine.

Once the employee has mastered all the facets of the job, he or she can begin to look forward to a promotion. The key, mail, or information clerk may be advanced to room clerk, then to assistant front office manager, and from there to front office manager, assistant manager (possibly specializing in a particular area of operations), and general manager. Once again it must be noted that the possibility of promotion to a managerial position is greatly enhanced by additional education in areas relating to the hotel and motel field. So important is this that some hotels and hotel chains offer financial assistance to outstanding employees to enable them to acquire college training in hotel management. In addition, some large hotels offer on-the-job training programs. These programs generally consist of a schedule of rotation, by which the trainee works for a period of time in each of the hotel's departments, thus acquiring a working knowledge of every area of the hotel's operation.

Promotion of housekeepers generally operates on the same basis as that of managers. One may begin as a floor housekeeper, be promoted to assistant housekeeper, and from there obtain promotion to the position of executive housekeeper. Although additional education may be helpful, it is not quite as important in this area as it is in the managerial area. It should not, however, be overlooked. There is only one executive housekeeper in a hotel, and when this position becomes vacant, the hotel's management will fill it with the person it considers best qualified and most dedicated. Both at that time and subsequently, during the performance of the duties of the executive housekeeper, education will prove most valuable.

Hotel and motel chains offer better opportunities for advancement than independent hotels. In these organizations, employees may not only rise within the individual hotel itself, but may transfer to other hotels and motels as openings occur. There is also the possibility of obtaining a position at the chain's central office, an opportunity which may well lead to an executive position in the corporation.

If one does not wish to remain an employee, there is the possibility of opening one's own hotel or motel. There are thousands of such operations across the United States. These afford their owners a comfortable living and a source of considerable satisfaction.

GETTING A JOB AS A HOTEL OFFICE WORKER

Although some knowledge of bookkeeping and some typing skill are helpful, most of the actual skills necessary for proficiency in hotel office work are taught on the job.

What is of most concern to employers is an indication that an applicant will be able to perform well in that area of the job in which aptitude, more than skill, determines success.

A hotel door is always open and anyone may walk in. A hotel office worker's primary ability must be that of being able to deal with the public. This may include discussing a discrepancy in the bill with an individual, or contending with a busload of conventioneers arriving at one o'clock in the morning. A hotel office worker must not only be able to handle these situations calmly, but all others which may occur as well.

Because many large hotels have a considerable number of guests from abroad, the ability to speak a foreign language is considered by many employers to be an important asset.

SALARY, BENEFITS, AND WORKING CONDITIONS

Hotels and motels are generally clean, air conditioned, and basically pleasant places in which to work. The main disadvantage is in the fact that they are open twenty-four hours a day. This means that there is a considerable amount of night work, and newly hired employees are often put on the night shift.

In large cities, hotel employees are usually union members. The starting salary for a unionized hotel office worker is approximately $175. In addition, employees receive the standard union benefits, which include a specified number of sick days, paid vacations, medical coverage, and pensions. The salary and benefits in non-union hotels vary greatly, depending upon the size of the establishment, whether or not it is part of a chain, and its location. Hotel manager trainees may expect between $9000 and $13,000 per year, with periodic increases during the first year or two.

7 The POSTAL CLERK

Postal clerks sort incoming and outgoing mail and provide window services and information.

In 1639, all mail coming into the English colonies was delivered to a "tavern." The tavern keeper was, in effect, the postmaster, and he kept the mail until it was called for.

Today there are more than 30,000 post offices throughout the United States and its territories and possessions. These offices may range in size from those no larger than a corner in a rural store, in which the postmaster is the only employee, to those in large cities, in which thousands of people are employed. Whatever size, every post office is headed by a postmaster and staffed by clerks. There are basically two categories of clerks: **distribution clerks** and **window clerks**.

Distribution clerks, comprising the majority of the clerks employed by the post office, sort incoming and outgoing mail. Some operate the various machines which, presently, sort approximately 50 percent of the mail; the other 50 percent is separated by hand.

Window clerks sell stamps, postcards, and money orders, accept letters and parcels, and perform the other services in which a customer is directly involved.

In very small post offices, one clerk may be the distribution clerk, the window clerk and, as mentioned earlier, the postmaster as well.

WHAT DOES A POSTAL CLERK DO?

Distribution clerks are responsible for the movement of mail. When mail arrives at the post office, it is separated into groups (letters, parcel post, magazines, newspapers) by machines operated by clerks and mail handlers. The letters are fed into a stamp-canceling machine. The rest of the mail is canceled by hand. All of the canceled mail is then moved to another section of the post office for sorting by destination. If the office is equipped with a ZMT (ZIP Mail Translator), the clerk operating this machine reads the ZIP code on each letter as the machine picks it up and then presses on the machine's keyboard the button which corresponds to the letter's destination; the letter then drops into the correct slot. In offices where the ZMT is not in use, clerks must separate the mail by hand into primary destination categories: mail for the local area, for each nearby state, for groups of distant states, and for some of the largest cities. Following this primary distribution is one or more secondary distributions: for example, local mail is often combined with mail which has come in from other cities and then sorted according to street and number.

Depending upon the size of the post office, the window clerk may be considered either a **specialized clerk** or a **general clerk.** Window clerks sell stamps and money orders, check packages to make sure that their condition is satisfactory for mailing, and then weigh them to determine postage. They insure and register mail and answer questions regarding postage rates, mailing restrictions, and other postal matters. Window clerks also assist customers who wish to file a claim for a damaged package, and they deal with incoming and outgoing foreign mail and the customs restrictions applying to those letters and packages. In a large post office, a window clerk may work as a registry clerk, for example, and do nothing else; in a small post office, a window clerk may perform all the functions.

On a more general level, there are certain things that the Post Office requires of its clerks (as well as all of its other personnel).

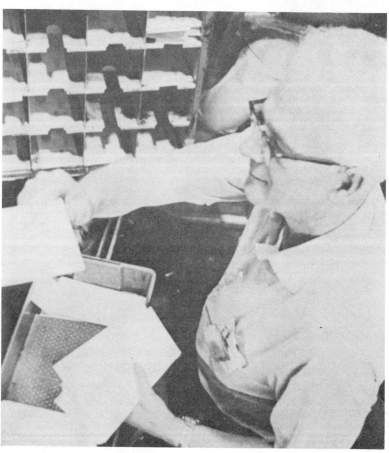

The distribution clerk at work.

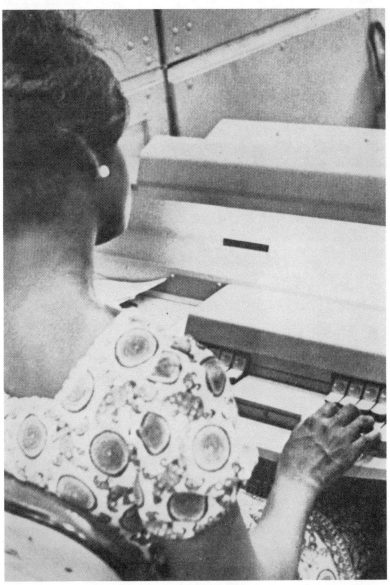

The operator distributes mail by using an electro-mechanical sorting machine.

Accuracy: In order to provide customers with the best possible service, all functions must be handled accurately.

Production: As in all other business, the relation between production and cost is also important to the Post Office.

Following orders and instructions: The supervisor is responsible for controlling and directing the clerks' work. Following instructions and carrying out orders is part of the clerk's job, and failure to do so is a serious matter.

Permission to leave the work area: The supervisor must know the whereabouts of the clerks at all times. A clerk may not leave his place of assignment without first obtaining his supervisor's permission.

Punctuality and attendance: When a clerk is scheduled to work, it is important that he reports for duty and reports on time. Absence without official leave can result in disciplinary action as well as loss of pay. If a clerk is absent from duty because of illness or emergency, he should report as soon as possible by calling his work station.

Personal appearance and habits: All clerks, but especially those whose duties bring them into contact with the public, must be conscious of the fact that their conduct and appearance can affect the confidence of the public either favorably or unfavorably.

Safety: Clerks are expected to "think safety and act safely" in all of their assignments. This will ensure protection for the clerk and the mail.

Payment of just debts: Although the Post Office does not interfere in the private lives of employees, it does expect its employees to be honest, reliable, trustworthy, of good character and reputation, and to conduct themselves both during and outside of working hours, in a way that reflects favorably upon the postal service. Postal employees must pay all just financial debts. Complaints concerning nonpayment of debts create embarassment to the postal service and to the employee. Failure to pay just debts is a cause for disciplinary action.

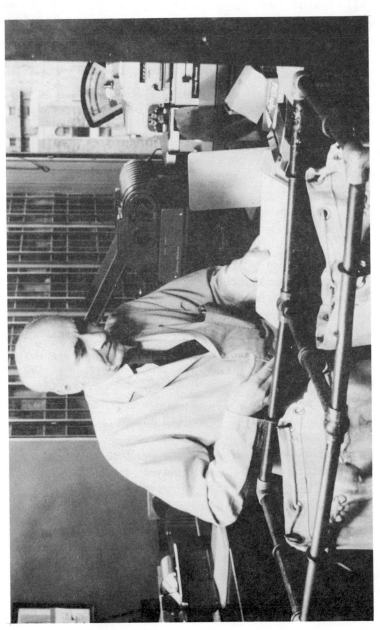

For purposes of speed and efficiency, metered mail is separated from stamped mail.

SKILLS AND PERSONALITY

The requirements for employment as a postal clerk do not include any specific personality traits; anyone is eligible to apply for work at the Post Office.

Applicants also do not have to have any specific skills. Any machine or equipment used is taught on the job. However, proficient postal clerks usually have a good memory, good coordination, and the ability to read rapidly and accurately.

Distribution clerks should be able to get along with other clerks and should be able to work unimpeded by the tension and strain of meeting deadlines. Window clerks must be tactful when dealing with the public, especially when answering questions or receiving complaints.

WHAT ARE THE OPPORTUNITIES?

The number of postal clerks is expected to change very little through the mid-1980's. Even though the amount of mail may increase along with population and business growth, modernization of post offices and installation of new automated equipment will increase the amount of mail each clerk can handle. Most new openings will occur as a result of the need to replace clerks.

Even though the outlook for initial employment is somewhat poor at the present time, opportunities for those who do secure positions are quite extensive.

All clerks are first hired as substitutes. The length of time required to advance from substitute to regular (full-time) clerk depends upon the "times" and the location. In larger urban centers, it currently takes from 1½ to 2 years before a substitute is appointed to a full-time position. The reason is that, when one becomes a substitute clerk, one's name is entered at the *bottom* of the substitute register; when a full-time clerk dies, retires, or moves to another position or occupation, his or her position is filled from the *top* of the substitute register, and a substitute clerk cannot become a regular clerk until his or her name moves to one of the first three positions on the register. The same procedure applies when new positions are filled.

Once one has become a clerk, either substitute or regular, all available positions within the Postal Service are open to that clerk. When a position becomes available (always a very specific position: the job, work hours, lunch period, etc., are all already set), it is posted in every post office in that area. Any employee is eligible to "bid" (apply) for the position, which is given to the "senior" (in terms of ability and length of service) applicant. For example, a distribution clerk would probably have to have approximately six or seven years experience in the postal service before having the seniority to be a successful bidder for the position of window clerk.

This system of bidding applies to *all* positions in the service. A clerk can just as easily move to another area as move up. Thus, a clerk might bid for a job as secretary, mechanic, computer technician, or any other position available and, if the clerk has the required skills, stand a fairly good chance of being awarded the job.

Advancement to supervisory levels works in much the same way. When a supervisory position becomes available, the job is posted and all interested employees submit applications for it. Written examinations are given, and the results of these are considered along with the applicant's job performance, record, and, most important, the result of an interview with the promotion advisory board.

Since nearly all occupations are needed in the Post Office, a clerk can move to another job without leaving the service. If, for example, a clerk decides to become a carpenter but does not have skills in that area, he can learn carpentry by attending classes (on his own time) at the Postal Employment Development Center and, when the skills have been developed, apply for the next available carpenter's job.

In general, the main requirements for advancement are: to have the necessary skills, take the job seriously, perform conscientiously, and enjoy working for the Post Office.

Although they are not actually opportunities, there are certain things which you may expect from your employer, the Post Office:

- Assistance. Clerks will be assisted in every way possible to gain and maintain the skills needed (including the operation of whatever machines are used on the job) in order to carry out duties quickly and safely.

- Fairness. All employees will be respected as adults, treated fairly and justly at all times, without discrimination of any kind.

- Evaluation. At scheduled intervals, each clerk's performance and behavior will be fairly evaluated by his or her supervisor. Outstanding performance as well as useful suggestions to improve the service are processed through the incentive awards system.

- Incentive and suggestion awards. Clerks may earn recognition for outstanding performance of duties, superior achievements for special acts or services which are over and above the normal work requirements. This recognition may be either a Superior Accomplishment Award (a one-time cash award) or a quality step increase (which places you in a higher earning category).

- Recognition for a suggestion which improves postal operations may be a letter of commendation, a certificate, or a cash award (up to $25,000), depending on the value of the idea.

GETTING A JOB AS A POSTAL CLERK

Applications for positions in the Post Office are accepted only when there is a need in the service for certain personnel. At these times, the fact is posted in all post offices. Interested job-seekers who are high school graduates or at least eighteen years of age submit an application and are then notified when the examination (in this case, the Clerk/Carrier Examination) will be given and at what location.

The examination consists of three parts: general intelligence (which counts for 40%), the ability to follow directions in the routing of mail (also 40%), and a memory test (20%). Interested applicants can study for this examination by purchasing one of the books currently available (i.e., *Post Office Clerk/Carrier Examination,* Arco Publishing Co., Inc.).

Merely passing the examination does not guarantee employment. Actually getting a job depends on how many people are needed, how many take the test, and the score achieved on the examination. These facts also determine the length of time you will have to wait before receiving an appointment. Currently, a score of 80% is considered a fair grade, and appointment is likely to come through in 1½ to 2 years. A grade of 75% or less will make it very unlikely that you will ever be called. If you achieve a grade of 90%, you can expect to be called in about six months. Certain adjustments in the scores are made for veterans. Five extra points are added to the score of an honorably discharged veteran, and ten extra points to the score of a disabled veteran or a veteran wounded in combat. Disabled veterans who have a compensable, service-connected disability of 10 percent or more are placed at the top of the register.

When a vacancy occurs, the three individuals at the top of the register are called for interviews and physical examinations. One of the three is then chosen to fill the vacancy as a substitute clerk. When a full-time position becomes available, the substitute is appointed to that position.

At the time of the interview, the potential clerk must fill out a number of forms (relating to past history, employment record, references). Usually, if the applicant has committed a crime or taken drugs, this will not be held against him if the circumstances are explained in a letter and if the interviewer is assured that no recurrence has taken place recently. If, however, the applicant does not mention a crime or makes a false statement regarding it, he will probably be dismissed when this is discovered. The Post Office does not run a check on applicants, but it does run a check on all new employees.

Postal clerks are classified as casual, part-time flexible, part-time regular, or full-time. **Casual** workers are hired to help when there is a large volume of mail to be moved, such as at Christmas. **Part-time flexible** workers do not have set work hours; they are called in to replace absent workers or to help when the work load warrants it. **Part-time regular** workers have definite work hours. Depending upon which position opens up, a substitute worker may be appointed to either a part-time regular or a full-time position.

SALARY, BENEFITS, AND WORKING CONDITIONS

Starting salary for postal clerks is approximately $5.75 per hour. Periodic raises are given until the top salary level is reached. It takes approximately eight years, broken down into twelve steps, for a clerk to attain the top salary of, presently, about $15,000 per year. An additional ten percent is paid to those clerks who work between 6 p.m. and 6 a.m.

Life insurance is provided from the first workday. The amount of the insurance equals the next thousand dollar increment above salary (i.e., if you earn $14,500 per year, you are given $15,000 worth of life insurance). Additional insurance is available for those clerks who request it.

The clerk is free to choose any health care plan available, and the Post Office will pay 75 percent of the annual premium.

In the Post Office, approved time off is called *leave*. The various kinds of leave are: annual leave (vacation), sick leave, military leave (for officially ordered military training), leave for personal affairs (charged against annual leave), and court leave (jury duty).

Annual leave is thirteen days per year for the first three years of employment, twenty days per year for the third through the fifteenth year of employment, and twenty-six days per year thereafter.

All postal employees are given two, regular days off per week (Sunday plus one other day).

Thirteen days of sick leave are allowed each year (accumulated at the rate of one hour of sick leave for every twenty hours worked). Sick leave can be accumulated indefinitely, thus affording protection from loss of income during a prolonged illness (if you have earned a sufficient amount of sick leave).

A pension is provided for each employee. A percentage of one's earnings is withheld each pay period to pay for this. Payroll savings plans are also available for those employees who wish to take advantage of them.

One of the greatest benefits for both education and advancement is the Postal Employment Development Center mentioned earlier.

8 The RECEPTIONIST
Switchboard and Office Machine Operators

Receptionists greet visitors, find out what they want, and refer them to the proper person in the organization.

Virtually every company in which clients, visitors, and other callers are received in an office has a receptionist. The receptionist, almost invariably a woman (97 percent of all receptionists), is usually the first person a visitor sees, and an important part of her job is making a good first impression.

Some receptionists are also responsible for operating the company's switchboard, called a PBX (*private branch exchange*). This is usually the case in smaller companies; large companies often have one or more PBX stations operated by full-time operators.

The receptionist may be responsible for operating some of the company's office machines, although this is rarely so if the receptionist is also the company's PBX operator. Again, however, large companies often have specialized personnel whose sole responsibility involves the operation of one or more of these machines.

WHAT DOES A RECEPTIONIST DO?

A receptionist may work either in the front office of a company or in the reception area of a particular department. The receptionist's desk is usually in an open room in which there are chairs for visitors. In some cases, however, she may be seated behind a wall or partition in which there is a window through which she may speak to visitors. (This is often so if she is also the PBX operator.)

In most offices, the receptionist's basic duty is to greet clients and other callers, find out what they want or whom they wish to see, and refer them to the proper person in the organization. This function generally involves calling or paging the person to be seen and telling him or her that there is a visitor waiting. The receptionist's work often involves diplomacy. If the person in the organization cannot or does not want to see the caller, it is up to the receptionist to explain, as tactfully as possible, why the person cannot be seen at this time.

If the receptionist is employed in a large plant or other operation in which security is a factor, the receptionist may have to provide the visitor with an identification badge and, possibly, an escort to take the visitor to the proper office or area. The receptionist, of course, keeps a record of the badge number and its return.

Receptionists who work for hospitals or doctors may be responsible for taking a patient's personal or case history and then directing the patient to the correct waiting or examination room.

Other duties usually performed by the receptionist include keeping a record of the names of callers, the time of arrival and departure, and the persons to whom they were referred. Receptionists may also be called upon to type, file, take and distribute telephone messages, make travel arrangements, do simple bookkeeping, handle the petty cash, and, as mentioned earlier, operate the switchboard.

SKILLS AND PERSONALITY

Someone wishing to pursue a position as a receptionist should have a high school diploma, a good command of spoken and written English, the ability to type at least 40 to 50 words per minute, a knowledge of elementary bookkeeping and general business procedures, some familiarity with filing, and spelling ability. If the particular position entails operation of the PBX, it will often be taught the beginner on the job. Any knowledge of this equipment which can be brought to the job, however, will be a definite advantage.

A receptionist should have a neat appearance, a pleasant voice, and an even disposition. She should be outgoing and like people and want to help them. A receptionist is usually not closely supervised; she must, therefore, have the common sense and understanding of the way a business is organized to allow her to deal with whatever situations arise.

WHAT ARE THE OPPORTUNITIES?

Few jobs in the clerical field are expected to grow faster than that of receptionist. Thousands of openings should become available through the 1980's as businesses expand and as receptionists are replaced. The position of receptionist is one of the few which will not be affected by automation. More and more, firms recognize the importance of the receptionist in establishing good public relations. The person-to-person nature of the receptionist's work is such that it can never be replaced by a machine.

In a fairly large company, a receptionist who has clerical skills may advance to a position as secretary or administrative assistant. This is especially possible if the company has a training program for its personnel or if the receptionist attends college or business school while working for the company. Opportunities in a small company are, however, rather limited.

WHAT DOES A PBX OPERATOR DO?

Although many PBX operators act as receptionists (as noted previously), the PBX duties themselves are the same regardless of whatever other duties the operator may have.

PBX operators connect interoffice or house calls, assist employees in making outgoing calls, supply information to callers, and record telephone charges. In small offices in which there are a limited number of telephones, the operator may, even if she does not act as receptionist, perform other office duties such as typing, sorting mail, taking and distributing messages, and filing.

The operation of the switchboard usually requires wearing a headset. Some switchboards are operated by dials or pushbuttons; with others, calls are placed by inserting and removing plugs that make switchboard connections.

SKILLS AND PERSONALITY

The basic requirements for becoming a PBX operator are a pleasant voice, good hearing, and the ability to sit for long periods in a fairly confined space.

Most PBX operators are trained on the job, often by telephone company operators. However, since many PBX operators must also perform other duties in the office (and since promotion may well depend upon proficiency in other areas), it is best to come to the position with such skills as typing, filing, elementary bookkeeping, general office practices, and, possibly, stenography.

WHAT ARE THE OPPORTUNITIES?

Although more small businesses will require PBX services in the future, employment of PBX operators is not expected to change significantly. The reason for this is the increasing use, among large companies, of CENTREX (*central exchange*), which enables calls to be made directly without an operator's assistance.

Although there are opportunities for advancement in large companies (to clerical, craft, or supervisory positions), possibilities for advancement in smaller companies tend to be limited.

PBX operators are generally concentrated in populated, urban areas such as New York, Chicago, and Los Angeles, and many of these are employed in manufacturing plants, hospitals, schools, and department stores.

WHAT DOES AN OFFICE MACHINE OPERATOR DO?

Various machines are currently being used in offices to speed the paperwork involved in operating a business. Some of these machines are operated by office personnel whose primary function is something else (such as receptionist). Some are used as a part of the primary job (such as a bookkeeper who uses adding and calculating machines). In other cases, personnel are hired specifically to operate a particular machine (such as a bookkeeping machine operator).

Some of the more common machine operating jobs are the following.

Billing machine operators prepare statements by typing information (such as name, item, and amount of sale) on a machine which automatically computes the customer's balance and required payments.

Mail preparing and mail handling machine operators use machines which prepare statements and letters for mailing and open incoming mail. Some of these machines may be 12 or 15 feet in length and are capable of folding and inserting a number of enclosures and then sealing the enve-

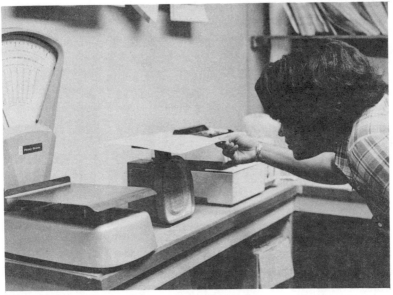

The office machine operator weighs the letter...

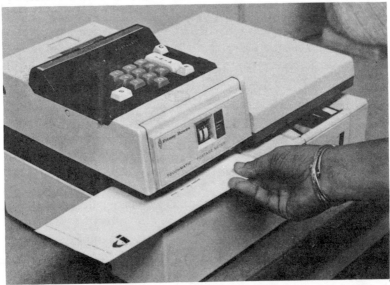

...and then inserts it in the postage meter.

lopes. Other machines address, stamp, and (if it is not done by the inserting machine) seal the envelope.

Embossing machine operators use machines which stamp names and addresses on metal plates. These stencils are then used in addressing machines.

Duplicating machine operators are employed in the use of mimeograph, stencil, and copying machines.

Tabulating machine operators operate machines that sort and total large amounts of accounting and statistical information and print the results on special business forms.

SKILLS AND PERSONALITY

Regardless of the type of machine operated, finger dexterity, good eye-hand coordination, and good vision are important. Those who operate billing and calculating machines should be reasonably proficient in simple arithmetic, thus they will be able to detect any obvious errors. Some mechanical ability will be helpful to those operating duplicating and tabulating machines.

Although some instruction is usually given on the job (the amount depending upon the complexity of the machine to be operated), most newly hired workers are expected to have a high school or business school diploma and to be able to type and operate adding machines and calculators. On-the-job training may consist of a few days' instruction in the office, or it may be a few weeks' training at a school run by the equipment manufacturer.

WHAT ARE THE OPPORTUNITIES?

Due to the growth of computerized record keeping and data processing systems, the number of employees needed specifically for the operation of office machines is expected to grow rather slowly through the 1980's.

Once one does have a job, however, the opportunities for advancement are fairly good. Promotion may be either to a more complex machine job, to a related clerical position, to a job involving the training of beginning machine workers, or to a supervisory position. An employer who considers an employee worthy of promotion will also usually provide whatever additional training is necessary.

SALARY, BENEFITS, AND WORKING CONDITIONS

The average salary for a beginning receptionist is $120 per week. This figure may be slightly higher if the receptionist also operates the company's switchboard. The wage for a beginning PBX operator is approximately the same as that for a receptionist.

Office machine operators are generally classed as follows:

Class A: very experienced; performing comparatively difficult work.

Class B: somewhat experienced; performing more routine tasks on simpler equipment.

Class C: little or no experience; given only routine assignments.

The salary given to an office machine operator reflects the category in which he or she has been placed based on experience and proficiency. For example, a Class A tabulating machine operator earns approximately $200 per week; a Class B tabulating machine operator earns approximately $170 per week; and a Class C operator earns approximately $140 per week.

Working conditions and benefits are basically the same for these positions as they are for most other office occupations.

In most cases, workers receive a specified number of "sick days," and two weeks paid vacation after having worked for one year. Longer vacations, usually based on the length of employment, may range up to four weeks or more.

Most companies offer pension plans, profit sharing plans, payroll savings plans, major medical coverage, and other forms of insurance.

Many organizations have, or are instituting, educational assistance programs which allow the employee to continue his or her education totally or partially at the company's expense.

Average earnings, switchboard operator-receptionists, March-September, 1976	
Atlanta, Ga.	$ 150.00
Baltimore, Md.	139.50
Billings, Mont.	118.50
Binghamton, N.Y.-Pa.	116.00
Boston, Mass.	147.50
Chattanooga, Tenn.-Ga.	130.50
Chicago, Ill.	153.50
Cincinnati, Ohio-Ky.-Ind.	138.00
Corpus Christi, Tex.	120.50
Daytona Beach, Fla.	116.50
Fresno, Calif.	139.50
Gainesville, Fla.	117.00
Green Bay, Wis.	135.50
Greensboro-Winston-Salem-High Point, N.C.	127.00
Greenville-Spartanburg, S.C.	125.50
Nassau-Suffolk, N.Y.	134.50
New York, N.Y.-N.J.	155.50
Northeast Pennsylvania	128.50
Oklahoma City, Okla.	130.00
Paterson-Clifton-Passaic, N.J.	136.50
Portland, Oreg.-Wash.	142.50
Poughkeepsie, N.Y.	140.00
Providence-Warwick-Pawtucket, R.I.-Mass.	127.50
Richmond, Va.	127.50
Stamford, Conn.	160.00
Syracuse, N.Y.	136.50
Trenton, N.J.	145.00

Excerpted from *Occupational Earnings and Wage Trends in Metropolitan Areas, 1976;* U.S. Department of Labor, Bureau of Labor Statistics.

9 The SECRETARY

Secretaries type, take dictation, deal with callers, open and route mail, answer the telephone, write reports, compose letters, and do research.

Behind every successful executive is an efficient secretary. This may not be a famous quotation, but it is no less true for that. Every organization depends upon secretaries to keep business running smoothly. Forget the jokes about the secretary who does nothing all day except file her nails and take coffee breaks. Although there are a few of these, the truth is that there are very few, and their jobs don't last very long. A secretary's role is much too demanding for this kind of behavior to go unnoticed and uncorrected. On the other hand, because a secretary is so important to the smooth running of a business, an efficient secretary is appreciated and rewarded.

Whether a secretary works for a single individual or two or three, or as a member of a secretarial pool (a group of secretaries, each of whom may be assigned to any manager or department head who needs a secretary at that time), she or he is at the center of communications within the firm. It is the secretary's responsibility to see that the proper message, containing correct information, is transmitted to the right person at the right time. In a large organization, or a small one, this is no easy task.

The secretarial pool functions as a communications center.

Secretarial work is traditionally considered a female occupation (in this discussion, the secretary will be referred to in the feminine), but even though approximately 80 percent of all secretaries are women, there are quite a number of excellent secretarial opportunities for men. In fact, because some male executives believe they could relate better to another man, they would prefer to have a male secretary; they don't only because so few men go into the secretarial field, making competent male secretaries difficult to find.

WHAT DOES A SECRETARY DO?

A person employed in a secretarial pool may be called upon by anyone in the company (usually at the managerial level) authorized to use a secretary's services. The duties may entail taking dictation, general typing, and transcribing from a dictating machine.

Administrative Secretary

In some companies, one secretary may work for three or four administrators. In such cases, all typing and dictation are handled in "word processing centers," thus the administrative secretary has more time to spend on other secretarial duties. This additional time allows her to work for more than one member of the administrative staff. Because the administrative secretary works for specific individuals in the organization, she is not considered part of the secretarial pool; however, three or four administrative secretaries usually share one area, and are thus able to help each other. If, for example, one has a great deal of work and another has very little, they can share the work, thus relieving the pressure on the "swamped" secretary as well as ensuring that the work is done on time. A beginning administrative secretary is usually assigned the routine chores of answering the telephone, taking and distributing messages, sorting and routing mail, and filing. One who is more experienced—or who has limited experience but shows a particular aptitude for more difficult work—is often called upon to fulfill more responsible tasks such as composing letters, writing reports, or doing research.

Private Secretary

A private secretary has the most demanding (and best paid) position in the secretarial community. In addition to her responsibility for the tasks (taking dictation, typing, composing letters, etc.) also performed by other secretaries, the private secretary has a number of added burdens. She must "screen" callers, both those who call on the telephone and those who come in person. She must decide, often without being able to consult her boss, who he or she will want to see and who should be put off for the time being or turned away altogether. A good private secretary realizes that her boss's most valuable asset is time, and she must be able to help him allot it so that the best possible use is made of the time available. In her boss's absence, a private secretary may have to make decisions—naturally, not major decisions regarding corporate policy, but decisions which, nonetheless, can adversely or advantageously affect some aspect of the business. To do this, she must act as she thinks her boss would act if he were available; thus, she must have a fair amount of insight as well as a practical knowledge of the firm's operations. But even this is not the extent of a private secretary's duties: there are also the peripheral, but no less important, duties such as making plane or hotel reservations, planning conferences, and arranging accommodations for visitors. The list is not endless but it is quite extensive.

Specialists

There are also secretaries who specialize. The **technical secretary** helps scientists or engineers write reports and research proposals. **Medical secretaries** write case histories and prepare medical reports. **Legal secretaries** assist attorneys in preparing briefs and doing legal research. Another area of specialization is the **social secretary.** She is responsible for arranging social functions, sending and answering personal correspondence, and informing her employer of pertinent social events. All of these careers require a considerable amount of specific training, but they also afford an individual whose basic skills are in the secretarial field to concentrate in a particular area in which she is interested.

Whether one is a member of the secretarial pool, a private secretary, or a specialist, working in the secretarial field puts one at the nerve center of the organization.

SKILL/PERSONALITY CHECKLIST

The following questions are designed to help you evaluate whether or not your abilities and personality indicate an aptitude for a position in the secretarial field. This is not, however, the last word; you should merely regard the result as an indication of your *present* status in relation to this position. This is not a test which you will either pass or fail. Answer the questions honestly, as your answers will help you determine the most suitable course for your future.

Respond to the questions in the following manner: **1** = little or no skill; **2** = moderate skill; **3** = superior skill. The questions relating to personality cannot, of course, be answered on the basis of skill; respond to them numerically, as the others, on the basis of degree (**1**= little or none; **2** = moderate; **3** = superior).

A total of between **14** and **23** indicates little or no aptitude for secretarial work; **24-33**, moderate aptitude; **34-42**, superior aptitude.

☐ Can you type?

☐ Can you take shorthand (in any system)?

☐ Do you have any familiarity with filing systems?

☐ Are you proficient in simple math?

☐ Do you have any knowledge of records' control?

☐ How good is your command of English (verbal and written)?

☐ Do you enjoy helping people solve problems?

☐ Are you basically a cheerful person?

☐ Are you methodical; a good planner and organizer?

☐ Do you prefer indoor to outdoor work?

☐ Do you prefer a job in which you remain seated most of the day?

☐ Would you feel "put upon" if you were asked to perform a comparatively menial chore (such as emptying a wastebasket or making coffee)?

☐ Do you feel that you are loyal?

☐ Do you consider yourself a "nine-to-five" type of person (one who would resent having to work overtime or on an occasional Saturday)?

SKILLS AND PERSONALITY

Typing is not the most important part of a secretary's job, but it is the primary skill necessary for getting that first secretarial position. Almost anyone can learn to type, and the faster you can type—not forgetting accuracy—the easier you will find getting a job. Forty words per minute (WPM)—with no more than one error—is the absolute minimum acceptable for civil service positions. However, to get a fairly nice job in private industry, you should be able to type at least 55-60 WPM. If you can type 75 or more WPM, you should have no trouble at all finding quite a good job, even if you have just graduated from high school and have no prior experience.

There are a number of **shorthand** systems; some use the conventional alphabet, some use symbols, and some require the use of a machine. Gregg shorthand is the most widely used system, but knowlege of any system will be an asset. (If you are the only one in the office taking dictation, you will probably be allowed to use any system; however, if there are a number of secretaries, you will, in most cases, be required to learn the system used by the rest of the people in the department.) The civil service minimum for shorthand is 80 WPM; 100 WPM will help you get a nice, entry-level position; the ability to take dictation at over 100 WPM will enable you to get a good job and a salary equal to your worth.

An example of Gregg shorthand symbols.

Filing is part of every secretary's job. It is not absolutely necessary for you to know everything about filing, but a basic familiarity with numerical (the Dewey decimal system) or alphabetical filing systems will undoubtedly count in your favor.

Math and **bookkeeping** are not major parts of a secretary's job, but you may, at some time, be called upon to perform in these areas. It is thus wise to sharpen your skills in simple math and acquire an elementary knowledge of bookkeeping procedures.

Records' control is simply a matter of checking figures and keeping track of records (invoices, bills, etc.). Arithmetic proficiency and knowledge of filing will help you in this area.

Command of **English** is extremely important, especially if you hope one day to become a private secretary. But even below this level, it is essential that you have the ability to make yourself understood in both verbal and written communications. If private secretary is your goal, or if you plan to specialize, you will be expected to write letters and reports which will be clearly understood.

Your disposition will play a major role in your success as a secretary. If you are cheerful and can enjoy performing routine duties as well as assisting in important matters, you will find the secretarial world quite a pleasant one.

Your boss will expect you to know where everything is and when everything is to happen. This is not always possible, but keeping things in order will be much easier if you develop methodical habits and are able to organize work and time to the best possible advantage.

A secretary works indoors at a desk; there is no way of getting around that fact.

Loyalty and an uncomplaining attitude toward overtime will help you find pleasure and fulfillment in a secretarial position. A secretary must feel a certain amount of loyalty and identification with her boss. Without these qualities, there will be little or no interest, and without interest, the job will become drudgery. A cheerful acceptance of occasional overtime will make you feel more comfortable in your job; overtime work is sometimes necessary, and if you have ill feelings about it, the chances are that they will taint the pleasanter aspects of the job.

WHAT ARE THE OPPORTUNITIES?

Among the other things causing businesses to move out of the large cities (notably New York) is the fact that good office workers, particularly secretaries, are so difficult to find. This condition makes the field, in effect, a sellers' market; if you are proficient in typing, stenography, and the other secretarial skills, you have a valuable product to sell and a ready market in which to sell it. But you must have the skills, otherwise you are merely one more reason for employers to move to other areas.

Although a beginning secretarial job may start you on the road to private secretary or some field of specialization, it may also act as a stepping-stone to a managerial or executive position. A really good private (or executive) secretary should know very nearly as much about the business as her boss, and if she has worked her way through the ranks, she will know it from the bottom-up; these are both excellent recommendations for promotion.

Another way of moving up in an organization is to travel along with your boss. If you have made your assistance valuable to a rising manager, he or she will take you along when promoted. This kind of opportunity will, of course, bring added responsibilities and an increase in salary, but it should also bring increased diversity and the chance to tackle new problems.

Of interest to experienced secretaries as well as beginners are the training programs which many private firms and government agencies have instituted. Through these programs, working secretaries can upgrade their skills. For the beginner, the benefit is in being able to learn while working. An untrained person will be hired for a fairly low-level position, but will spend a part of each working day attending classes. After completing the course, if she has done well, she will be promoted.

A further note of importance is the growing number of opportunities for part-time and temporary secretarial workers. This is, of course, of interest to women who may wish to continue working on a part-time basis while raising a family, but it may also be an important consideration to a person who wishes to continue his education or pursue some other interest while working.

Employment in the secretarial field is expected to increase more rapidly than the average for all occupations during the next five to ten years. This will occur mainly as those companies which already have large secretarial staffs enlarge their operations; such organizations include banks, insurance companies, and all facets of the recreation industry, as well as state, local, and federal government agencies.

Regardless of the introduction in recent years of many new types of automatic office equipment, employment of secretarial workers is not expected to be adversely affected. However, those secretaries who are familiar with these machines will find their prospects in the future considerably broader than those who have not acquainted themselves with the equipment.

GETTING A JOB AS A SECRETARY

As noted previously, some firms offer training programs; most companies, however, prefer to hire someone who already has the necessary skills. Each company has its own "way" of doing things and is willing to teach the new employee the particular procedures used, but they want someone who has the basic knowledge.

There are a number of ways in which you can develop your secretarial skills while still in high school. You may plan a schedule of intensified home study, or take business classes at an occupational training center or a recognized business school. Another alternative is a part-time job in which you can sharpen your skills and in which you are not expected to perform quite as well as you would under full-time conditions.

Specialization requires special training. If you plan to go into legal, medical, or technical secretarial work, you must have the proper educational background.

Once you have gotten a job, you can increase your skills and broaden your knowledge of the company's operations by taking the courses (if any) offered by the company or by taking night classes at a local college or university. Many companies will pay for continuing education if the classes are job-related. This is an important benefit, and something you should ask about when applying for a job.

During the course of your secretarial career, you may feel ready to take the series of examinations offered by the National Secretaries Association. Passing these tests will entitle you to the designation of C.P.S. (Certified Professional Secretary). Increasingly, this designation is recognized by employers as a mark of achievement and excellence in the secretarial field.

SALARY, BENEFITS, AND WORKING CONDITIONS

Starting salary for a secretary with no shorthand skills ranges from $150 to $175 per week; with shorthand training you should be able to expect a weekly salary of $165 to $190 per week. These are considered base salaries and can do nothing except increase as you gain knowledge and experience. Specialization and great proficiency in typing or stenography will allow you to demand a higher wage.

Benefits vary from company to company and should be considered before you accept employment. Many firms offer pension plans, profit sharing plans, payroll savings plans, major medical coverage, and other forms of insurance.

Most companies work a 40-hour week, except in the Northeast, where the standard work week is 35 hours. In most cases, workers receive seven or more paid holidays per year, a specified number of "sick days," and two weeks paid vacation after having worked for one year. Longer vacations, usually based on the length of employment, may range up to four weeks or more.

Average earnings, secretaries, March-September, 1976	
Atlanta, Ga.	$191.00
Baltimore, Md.	187.50
Billings, Mont.	160.00
Binghamton, N.Y.-Pa.	202.50
Boston, Mass.	191.00
Chattanooga, Tenn.-Ga.	162.00
Chicago, Ill.	196.00
Cincinnati, Ohio-Ky.-Ind.	184.50
Corpus Christi, Tex.	172.00
Daytona Beach, Fla.	169.50
Fresno, Calif.	180.00
Gainesville, Fla.	159.00
Green Bay, Wisc.	168.00
Greensboro-Winston-Salem-High Point, N.C.	170.50
Greenville-Spartanburg, S.C.	156.00
Nassau-Suffolk, N.Y.	182.00
New York, N.Y.-N.J.	207.00
Northeast Pennsylvania	156.50
Oklahoma City, Okla.	169.50
Paterson-Clifton-Passaic, N.J.	188.50
Portland, Ore.-Wash.	187.00
Providence-Warwick-Pawtucket, R.I.-Mass.	158.50
Richmond, Va.	172.00
Stamford, Conn.	209.00
Syracuse, N.Y.	191.00
Trenton, N.J.	193.00

Excerpted from *Occupational Earnings and Wage Trends in Metropolitan Areas, 1976;* U.S. Department of Labor, Bureau of Labor Statistics.

10 The STENOGRAPHER, The TYPIST

The stenographer takes dictation by hand or by machine and then types the dictation. Typists transcribe taped dictation and type letters and other material.

Business today is conducted almost exclusively on the basis of written communications, and virtually all written communications are typed: letters, contracts, notes of meetings, even inter-office memos. Whether a company is large or small, a typist (even one hired on a part-time basis) and perhaps a stenographer, are indispensable to the communications network which keeps a company in touch with its own operations and with other companies.

Stenographers take dictation and then transcribe what they have written. There are a number of different shorthand systems (in addition to shorthand machines), and a stenographer must know one of these as well as being able to type. Naturally, a stenographer does not spend all of her time taking dictation and typing. In fact, on the average, most stenographers spend only one third of the workday actually taking dictation. The remainder of the time may be spent on any of a number of other tasks which the stenographer is assigned.

Aside from any other duties she may perform in the office, a **typist** types. She may be part of a typing pool, transcribe taped dictation on a full-time basis, work for an individual or a group, type finished copies of rough drafts, or operate high-speed typing equipment.

Although stenography and typing are traditionally considered careers for women, there is a place for men in these areas, and it is an exceptionally good place. Especially in the areas of finance, real estate, transportation, and heavy industries, many male executives prefer to have their clerical work done by male stenographers and typists. This preference is often based on the fact that the executives feel that men will more easily understand the technical terms used in these fields. As erroneous as this may be, it is an attitude which may be put to good advantage by a man pursuing a career in this area. Because so few men enter this area, there are very few who are truly capable, and these men often advance quite rapidly.

WHAT DOES A STENOGRAPHER DO?

Stenographers take dictation using either one of the many shorthand systems (of which *Gregg* is the most widely known) or a stenotype machine which, much like a typewriter, prints symbols as keys are pressed.

The dictation taken may be nothing more than a short memo, or it may be a letter. Stenographers also very often take notes during meetings, conferences, hearings, and the proceedings of state and federal legislatures.

The **general stenographer**, a designation which includes most beginners, takes routine dictation such as letters and memos and types the notes taken. In the case of a letter, the rough draft is often given back to the person who dictated the letter. That person then makes whatever changes or corrections seem necessary. The letter may then either be given back to the stenographer for final typing, or it may be given to a typist. In addition to these tasks, the general stenographer usually performs other office tasks such as filing, answering the telephone, acting as receptionist, opening and directing mail, and operating office machines.

More **experienced stenographers**, if they have shown an aptitude for it, take more difficult dictation. This may include giving a summary of a meeting on which the stenographer has sat in, or giving a word-for-word account of the proceedings. The skilled and experienced stenographer may also be called upon to compose or, while taking dictation, to "co-author" the correspondence being dictated. Such a position may also entail acting as supervisor, overseeing the activities of other stenographers, typists, or clerical workers.

Some stenographers specialize in a particular field, such as law, medicine, or engineering. These stenographers, called **technical stenographers**, must be familiar with the terms used in the particular field they have entered. A career as a technical stenographer requires additional education in the area of specialization.

Stenographers who are extremely proficient in a foreign language take dictation in that language. Others work as **public stenographers** and take dictation from anyone who happens to need a stenographer.

All of these positions usually entail taking dictation by hand. Although a stenotype machine may be used to record the proceedings of a meeting, most individuals prefer to speak to a stenographer who works with a pad rather than one who sits at a machine.

The stenotype machine is, however, widely used by **shorthand reporters.** These are stenographers who specialize in taking down everything said during proceedings. Almost half of the shorthand reporters currently working are court reporters. The court reporter records all statements and testimony made during a hearing or trial; this record is then considered the official transcript.

Other shorthand reporters, called "free-lance" reporters, work for themselves. They may take down out-of-court testimony for an attorney or record the activities of meetings, conferences, or conventions.

Most stenographers transcribe their own notes. In some cases, however, the notes are turned over to a typist who transcribes the record. Needless to say, the typist must know stenography to be able to read the symbols.

WHAT DOES THE TYPIST DO?

Junior typists, the point at which most typists begin in an organization, copy handwritten or rough drafts of letters or memos, type headings on form letters, and address envelopes. The junior typist may also perform other tasks such as filing, answering the telephone, and operating office machines. Except for the fact that the junior typist's main job is typing, this position is very similar to that of clerk typist, which combines typing with other general office work.

Senior typists perform tasks requiring considerable accuracy and judgment. They may type from handwritten drafts which are difficult to read or which contain technical material. In addition, they may lay out and type statistical tables and coordinate and prepare material from various sources which must be combined in a master to be copied.

Other typists, as mentioned earlier, may work from stenographic notes, and still others may transcribe dictation from dictating machines (cassette, belt, tape, or disc).

Some large companies in which there is a great amount of typing to be done have installed word processing centers. In these companies, typists are grouped together in one area in which all the transcribing and typing is done. These typists, called **correspondence secretaries**, often use high-speed typewriters, many of which are equipped with a programmed memory which allows a final copy to be produced with a minimum of retyping.

SKILLS AND PERSONALITY

Although a stenographer must be able to take dictation, it is something which almost anyone can learn and it is not considered the critical factor for a career. The most important aspect of stenography is **learning to transcribe correctly**. The reason this is considered critical is that it involves a knowledge of English usage, spelling, and punctuation.

The stenographer is more than just a machine which takes down the spoken word. Language, fully as much as the command of the shorthand system, is the tool of the trade. A stenographer must know where a comma belongs, but she must also know why it belongs there, just as she must know how to spell.

Stenographic and typing speed are also important. If you have taken a business course in high school, you should, upon completion, be able to type 60 words per minute (WPM) and take dictation at about 120 WPM. Most people dictate at about 100 WPM, but, since you are writing what is being said, you must be able to keep ahead of the person speaking. If you have no particular preference, excellence in either typing or shorthand should determine which field will be best for you; the more proficient you are, the higher your salary will be and the more rapidly you will advance in that area.

Unless a situation exists in which you must fit in with the rest of the stenographic staff, most employers have no preference regarding which stenographic system you use. Fitting in, in this sense, has nothing to do with personality; it deals with the fact that all the stenographers in an office must use the same system in case one is absent and another must transcribe or read her notes. What most employers consider paramount are speed, accuracy, and language proficiency.

Naturally, if you plan to enter a specialized area of stenography, additional skills will be required (the legal, medical, or engineering training mentioned earlier). This is also true if you plan on becoming a shorthand reporter, although in this case the additional skill is additional speed. Shorthand reporters in the federal government must be able to take at least 175 WPM, and many other positions require that the stenographer be able to take more than 225 WPM. Also, many courts of law require that the court reporter be a Certified Shorthand Reporter (CSR); other courts will hire a reporter with the understanding that they will acquire certification within one year.

Most employers require that the stenographer have a high school diploma. In addition, the stenographer should have good hearing, the ability to concentrate amid distractions (an especially important factor for shorthand reporters), poise, alertness, and a pleasant personality.

Typists must be able to type 40 to 50 WPM for an entry-level position. If you can type faster, you will be able to get a better job initially and, as your speed increases, you will rise that much higher that much more rapidly. Knowledge of high-speed typing equipment will enable you to get a job as a correspondence secretary or, at the least, put you in line for such a position when one becomes available. Transcribing machine operators who type recorded dictation must have good hearing. All typists must be especially good in spelling, must be neat, accurate, and able to concentrate on a task.

Regardless of whether you plan to pursue a career as a typist or a stenographer, you should have a knowledge of general office procedures, filing, various office machines (Xerox, adding machine, recorder), handling mail properly, record keeping, and the use of a multiple-line telephone.

WHAT ARE THE OPPORTUNITIES?

Stenographers and typists are needed in virtually every business and government agency. Because of the increased use of dictating machines, however, the need for stenographers is expected to continue the decline of recent years. On the other hand, the need for skilled shorthand reporters is expected to increase. The need for typists will also continue to increase as business expands, bringing with it the enormous volume of paperwork to be done (despite such technological advances as the typewriter which types as you speak to it). The opportunities for typists familiar with high-speed equipment as well as for those able to handle duties other than typing should be quite good.

Many stenographers who increase their skills and knowledge of the business are promoted to secretarial positions, and from there may advance to a management position. Other opportunities for advancement include promotion to supervisor of the stenographic pool or manager of clerical operations. Stenographers who acquire the necessary skill and speed may become shorthand reporters.

Opportunities for advancement for typists who remain in the typing field are somewhat limited. A junior typist may be promoted to senior typist, and from there to supervisor or typist in the word processing center. Further advancement requires moving out of the typing field. Acquiring stenographic skill will help the typist to obtain a position as a secretary, and from there the road is the same as it would be for a stenographer promoted to that position.

GETTING A JOB AS A STENOGRAPHER OR TYPIST

As jobs for stenographers are somewhat limited, a person having stenographic and typing skills might do better to seek employment as a secretary. Jobs for shorthand reporters are available and expected to increase, but getting such a position requires additional skill and training.

Jobs for typists are quite plentiful. If you can type rapidly, neatly, and accurately, have a basic knowledge of general office operations, and are willing to take the job seriously, you should have little trouble in finding a position as a typist.

SALARY, BENEFITS,
AND WORKING CONDITIONS

The average salary for beginning stenographers is $500 to $550 per month. Skilled beginners in the field of shorthand reporting receive between $800 and $1000 per month, depending upon speed and regional location. The average salary for beginning typists is about $130 per week.

Most companies work a 40-hour week, except in the Northeast, where the standard work week is 35 hours. In most cases, workers receive seven or more paid holidays per year, a specified number of "sick days," and two-weeks paid vacation after having worked for one year. Longer vacations, usually based on the length of employment, may range up to four weeks or more.

Benefits vary from company to company and should be considered before you accept employment. Many firms offer pension plans, profit sharing plans, payroll savings plans, major medical coverage, and other forms of insurance.

An additional benefit in many large companies is the educational program. This may be nothing more than on-the-job training, which is in itself quite valuable and an aid to promotion. But the program may also include classroom training in the firm itself. Classes offered may range from brush-up classes in typing and stenography to instruction in computer programming. The company may also offer a program whereby an employee can take job-related classes at a local university, college, or vocational school and receive some compensation, have the entire tuition paid by the company, or even be given some time off to pursue or complete a course of study. This is one of the greatest benefits of working for a large organization; if such a program is available, you should take full advantage of it.

Average earnings, general stenographers, March–September, 1976

Atlanta, Ga.	$176.50
Baltimore, Md.	190.50
Billings, Mont.	168.00
Binghamton, N.Y.–Pa.	170.00
Boston, Mass.	170.00
Chattanooga, Tenn.–Ga.	134.50
Chicago, Ill.	171.50
Cincinnati, Ohio–Ky.–Ind.	152.50
Corpus Christi, Tex.	157.00
Fresno, Calif.	138.50
Gainesville, Fla.	147.50
Green Bay, Wis.	167.50
Greensboro–Winston-Salem–High Point, N.C.	181.00
Greenville–Spartanburg, S.C.	150.00
Nassau–Suffolk, N.Y.	143.50
New York, N.Y.–N.J.	161.50
Northeast Pennsylvania	135.50
Oklahoma City, Okla.	143.50
Paterson–Clifton–Passaic, N.J.	165.00
Portland, Oreg.–Wash.	164.00
Providence–Warwick–Pawtucket, R.I.–Mass.	126.50
Richmond, Va.	153.00
Stamford, Conn.	168.00
Syracuse, N.Y.	155.50
Trenton, N.J.	165.00

Excerpted from *Occupational Earnings and Wage Trends in Metropolitan Areas, 1976;* U.S. Department of Labor, Bureau of Labor Statistics.

SOURCES OF INFORMATION

The following publications and organizations can provide you with information and guidance.

1. The Bank Teller

Corns, Marshall C., *The Practical Operation and Management of a Bank.* 2 Vols., Bankers Publishing Co., 1962.

Chase Manhattan Bank
Teller Training Center
40 W. 34th St.
New York, N.Y. 10001

2. The Bookkeeper

Freeman, Hanna, and Kahn, *Bookkeeping and Accounting Simplified, Second edition.* Dallas: Gregg Publishing Division, McGraw-Hill Book Co., 1958.

Popham, Estelle and Ettinger, Blanche, *Opportunities in Office Occupations.* New York: Universal Publishing and Distributing Corp., 1972.

Ames Business School
2710 Broadway
New York, N.Y. 10025

3. The Cashier

Cashier Training Co., Inc.
165 W. 46th St.
New York, N.Y. 10036

4. The Clerk

Morrison, Phyllis, *A Career in the Modern Office,* New York: McGraw-Hill Book Co., 1970.

Popham, Estelle and Ettinger, Blanche, *Opportunities in Office Occupations.* New York: Universal Publishing and Distributing Corp., 1972.

Ames Business School
2710 Broadway
New York, N.Y. 10025

5. The Collection Worker

American Collectors Association
4040 W. 70th St.
Minneapolis, Minn. 55435

Associated Credit Bureaus
6767 Southwest Freeway
Houston, Texas 77036

North American Credit Corp.
One World Trade Center
Suite 2573
New York, N.Y. 10048

6. Hotel Office Personnel

The Educational Institute of the American Hotel and
Motel Association
1407 S. Harrison Rd.
East Lansing, Mich. 48823

National Executive Housekeepers Association, Inc.
Business and Professional Building
Gallipolis, Ohio 45631

New York Hotel and Motel School
721 Broadway
New York, N.Y. 10011

Council on Hotel, Restaurant, and Institutional Education
Suite 219, 11 Koger Executive Center
Norfolk, Va. 23502

7. The Postal Clerk

U.S. Post Office Department. *General Orientation Handbook for New Employees,* Handbook Series P-23, Part 220. Washington, D.C., June, 1969.
U.S. Post Office
Department of Employee Relations
General Post Office
New York, N.Y. 10001

8. The Receptionist: Switchboard and Office Machine Operators

Archer, Brecker, and Frakes, *General Office Practice,* Dallas: Gregg Publishing Division, McGraw-Hill Book Company, 1958.

U.S. Department of Labor. *Occupational Outlook Handbook,* Washington, D.C.: U.S. Government Printing Office, 1976-77.

9. The Secretary

Meehan, James R., Oliverio, Mary Ellen, and Pasewark, William, *Secretarial Office Practice.* Cincinnati: South-Western Publishing Co., Revised (8th Edition), 1972.

Ames Business School
2710 Broadway
New York, N.Y. 10025

National Secretaries Association (International)
2440 Pershing Road
Suite G10
Kansas City, Missouri 64108

10. The Stenographer and the Typist

Green, H.H., *Applied Dictation and Transcription.* New York: McGraw-Hill Book Company, 1957.

Popham, Estelle and Ettinger, Blanche, *Opportunities in Office Occupations.* New York: Universal Publishing and Distributing Corp., 1972.

"So You Want To Be a Stenographer," *Ford Career Guide No. 5,* Dearborn: Educational Affairs Department.

National Shorthand Reporters Association
25 W. Main St.
Madison, Wisconsin 53703